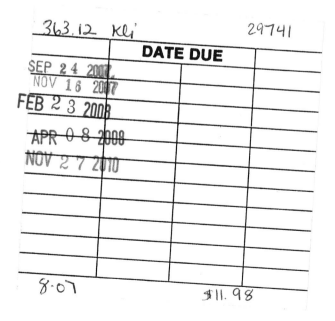

# EXIT ROW

*The True Story of an Emergency Volunteer,*
*a Miraculous Survivor and*
*the Crash of Flight 965*

Tammy Kling

SOURCEBOOKS, INC.®
NAPERVILLE, ILLINOIS

Published by Sourcebooks, Inc.
P.O. Box 4410, Naperville, Illinois 60567-4410
(630) 961-3900
FAX: (630) 961-2168
www.sourcebooks.com

Library of Congress Cataloging-in-Publication Data

Kling, Tammy L.
   Exit row: the true story of an emergency volunteer, a miraculous survivor and the crash of flight 965.
       p. cm.
   ISBN 1-57071-860-1 (Hardcover)
1. Aircraft accidents—Colombia—Buga Region (Valle del Cauca) 2. Survival after airplane accidents, shipwrecks, etc. 3. Search and rescue operations. I. Title.
   TL553.53.C7 K58 2002
   363.12'4'0986152—dc21

                                                                2002003623

Printed and bound in the United States of America
         LB   10   9   8   7   6   5   4   3   2   1

Dedicated to Benjamin and Mercedes Ramirez

# Acknowledgments

Thank you to Hillel Black, an extraordinary editor with a sharp sword and a discerning, creative mind, and to Peter Lynch, for making it all happen. To the employees of American Airlines and carriers across the world, for your ongoing professionalism and dedication to safe skies—the human element of the airline industry, which I have attempted to portray in this book. Although the media that follows a commercial airplane accident is always excessive, deaths on airplanes in the United States have averaged one hundred per year, compared to homicides, which average more than fifteen thousand, or automobile crashes, which claim more than forty thousand people annually. Finally, the most special thank you of all to Cita, for all that you are and will be to this world. Although it couldn't have been easy, you shared a bit of yourself so that this story could be told.

# Table of Contents

# Disclaimer

This story is a true and factual account of the author's own personal experiences and opinion surrounding the aftermath of a devastating plane crash and the Emergency Response Teams of commercial airlines. It is not intended to reflect the opinion of any airline carrier, its representatives, or any person associated with a specific airline, investigation, or aircraft incident. No information here is disclosed that could breach any security or safety program of any air carrier, nor is this book intended to portray the author as an expert in aviation. This is a personal account of an airline's Emergency Response Team activation. Actual names of survivors, airline personnel, and others have been replaced with pseudonyms out of respect for the privacy of those involved, and to protect the identity of certain individuals and entities. Certain facts, including those surrounding the training program and response team, as well as descriptions of individuals have been altered to ensure the integrity and confidentiality of any future Emergency Response Team operations. The royalties from this book will be donated to a children's charity for orphaned and abandoned children.

# Prologue

*"Feo! Malo!"*

The boy was just three, yet he yelled at me with the hatred of an adult. The words meant bad, and ugly—and if he were a grown man I know he would have killed me. The child spat at me, then ran for the shelter of his grandfather's arms.

Today, the toddler would be ten years old. I still think of him and wonder how his life turned out since the day he was orphaned, after the airplane that his parents and siblings were comfortably seated inside exploded into the side of a mountain just a few minutes before it would have landed. Nothing I could do or say could turn back time, and I will always remember the moment I realized that I was incapable of easing his pain.

I remember many things from that day. The child, in all his youth and innocence, didn't really know me. But he knew enough to understand that I was the mean lady from the airline, from his perspective, the same airline that took his mommy and daddy away. I remember the eeriness of the setting, how what was left of the little boy's family huddled together in the lobby of the bustling hotel in Colombia, where the airplane went down, against the backdrop of a Christmas festival. The air was alive with foreign music and the laughter of children. I remember buying lunch for the boy and his grandparents, two fragile beings whose own time on Earth was slipping away. I remember their faces, aging before me, etched with the misery that only a parent who is about to bury a child could know. I remember the stiff silence at our table at the edge of an oversized pool, where other children gaily splashed and shouted, and the stark contrast to the little boy in front of me.

I remember every detail from that day—how nothing went right, and the universe gave not even an inch. I remember how the table we dined at teetered unmercifully each time the grandfather reached for his glass of water and how no amount of matchbooks or paper scraps could repair it. I remember things that will stay with me forever, like the sorrow in the old man's eyes when he could bring himself to look at me, and the way his shoulders turned forward from the weight of losing his family. I remember thinking how destructive despair can be. The old man was without emotion, his eyes listless and yellowing.

And there are many things I'd like to forget. Like how the old man apologized for his grandson's behavior with compassionate words that made me sick to my stomach. And how I excused myself from the table to ride the elevator for who knows how long, until finally I exited on the sixth floor and vomited into a plant. I remember feeling unworthy of an apology and helpless to ease his pain.

This is a book about life. It is my hope that it will be a thought-provoking contribution to human knowledge about the airline industry and the people on all sides of a disaster, the crisis workers, survivors, and the family members of those who lost their lives to fate. More importantly, it is my desire to provide an awakening of what you already know to be true, that there is no time to waste. Destiny will have its way with each of us regardless of our carefully laid plans, hopes, and dreams.

Working a crash site as a member of an airline's Emergency Response Team (ERT) taught me a valuable lesson early in life. Just a few more minutes and the passengers flying from the United States to Latin America would have been safely on the ground, hugging their loved ones at the arrival gate. Two or three minutes, or even seconds, can forever alter the life you have made for yourself, and the plans and promises of tomorrow are just that. So whatever you strive for, do today without doubt, abandon, or hesitation. Whoever it is that you love, tell them today. Tomorrow may never come.

# chapter one

# El Deluvio

It was a route he had flown many times before. Miami to Cali was so routine that Captain Nicholas Tafuri had done nothing out of the ordinary to prepare for it. In the days leading up to the flight, he had spent time relaxing, playing tennis with his wife, and visiting family members in New Jersey.

Captain Tafuri and his copilot, first officer Don Williams, boarded the American Airlines 757 in Miami in a festive mood, anticipating the impending Christmas holiday. In the cockpit, they completed the standard preflight checks and prepared for takeoff, while 155 holiday travelers boarded the plane.

It was the twentieth of December 1995, and the airplane, a new Boeing 757 that American had purchased just four years prior, was scheduled to depart at 4:40 P.M. But the congested airport traffic delayed the takeoff, and Flight 965 departed Miami International two hours later, at 6:35 P.M.

The night sky was clear and it would be a smooth, three-hour journey to the Alfonso Bonilla Aragon International Airport in Cali, which was situated in an abundant valley forty-three miles long and twelve miles wide. As the airplane descended over the majestic Andean mountain range, the mood among the passengers in the cabin was jubilant. Their loved ones and family members would greet them, and the presents the passengers had carefully wrapped and stored in the overhead bins would be placed under Colombian Christmas trees. Thirty-five miles from landing, the airplane soared through clear skies over the peaks of El Deluvio, a large and looming mountain overlooking the massive jungle.

"We have begun our descent for landing at Cali," Captain Tafuri announced over the aircraft intercom. "It's a lovely evening as we had expected. I'd like to thank everyone for coming with us. Again, I apologize for being late tonight. These things do happen sometimes, very frustrating, but there wasn't very much we could do about it."

Minutes later, Flight 965 descended to 24,000 feet. The pilots radioed the control tower with their altitude and distance from the Cali airport. Tafuri and Williams had been trained to continually verify exact location of their aircraft, due to the unusually high terrain in Central and South America, and they did this several times. Outside the airplane windows, passengers observed a magnificent night sky dotted with stars, but they had no way of knowing that in the cockpit, something had gone terribly wrong.

"We got fucked up here didn't we?" Captain Tafuri asked the copilot. They were only minutes away from landing, but had somehow gotten turned around.

"Yeah," First Officer Williams responded.

"How did we get fucked up here?" the captain asked again.

Donnie Williams was an experienced copilot who had begun flying in college, after enrolling in the Air Force reserve officer training corps. On this night, Williams was manning the airplane controls while Captain Tafuri was in charge of the radio, sending messages to the control tower about their direction and coordinates. First Officer Williams had flown a variety of aircraft during his time in the Air Force, including trainers and fighters. He also served as an instructor in ground school, flight simulators, and jets, proving to be an exemplary pilot with an eye for detail. In 1985, he was awarded Air Force instructor of the year, and in the following year he began his career with American Airlines, logging thousands of miles in commercial planes. He had flown to Latin America often. The Boeing 757 they were flying had logged just over thirteen thousand miles, and not one Boeing 757 had ever been involved in a fatal accident.

In the cockpit, Captain Tafuri continued the exchange with the control tower in an effort to obtain direction.

"And American, uh, thirty-eight miles north of Cali, and you want us to go Tulua and then do the Rozo, uh, to the runway right?" he asked. "To runway one nine?"

The pilots had been assigned an arrival path that would take them past two waypoints, which would define the precise direction to the landing strip via radio-wave transmissions. These transmissions would act as a compass in the cockpit. Tulua would be the first waypoint, and Rozo would be the next, located just three miles from the airport.

"Niner six five you can land runway one niner," came the reply from the control tower. "What is your altitude and distance from Cali?"

In Colombia, a country with a turbulent history of civil wars, guerrilla activity had been rampant. Three years earlier, anti-government guerrillas had destroyed the only operable radar facility available to pilots landing in Cali. Normally, airplanes would be displayed on a controller's radar screen, eliminating reporting errors and communication mix-ups.

"Okay, we're thirty-seven miles DME [distance] at ten thousand feet," Captain Tafuri responded to the tower. "You're okay," the captain reassured Williams. "You're in good shape now."

*   *   *

In the terminal at Alfonso International airport, crowds were thick, as hundreds awaited the arrival of loved ones flying in for the holiday. In minutes, Flight 965 from Miami would be on the ground. As the aircraft continued its descent, Captain Tafuri transmitted several messages back and forth from the airplane to the control tower in an effort to find their bearings. At 9:41 P.M., the controller radioed the plane again, but this time his voice was filled with concern.

"Niner six five, altitude?"

The Cali airport was nestled between menacing mountains, the peaks of which had already claimed hundreds of lives in previous airplane crashes.

"Nine six five nine thousand feet," Captain Tafuri replied.

"Roger, distance now?" asked the controller.

There was no reply. The controller called to the airplane again, but there was only silence.

In the cockpit, the automatic terrain warning alarm sounded loudly. *Terrain, terrain, whoop, whoop!*

The pilots added power and pulled up, guiding the nose away from the ground towards the sky.

"Oh shit...." said Captain Tafuri. The noise in the cockpit was deafening. "Pull up, baby!"

The plane rolled and then stalled, activating the stick shaker.

"Up, up, up!" Captain Tafuri pleaded.

They were the last words captured on the cockpit voice recorder before the airplane struck the peaks of El Deluvio, the name given to the San Jose Mountain high in the Andes. The gigantic peaks had been named El Deluvio—the flood—by locals who believed an ancient legend that remnants of Noah's ark had been discovered there.

The plane soared uncontrollably over the ridge of the mountain, nearly eight thousand feet in the sky, shearing a path through the forest as it impacted, snapping treetops two hundred fifty feet from the top. Flight 965 cut a trail through the jungle and broke into pieces, sending tail and wing parts scattering across the earth into darkness. Within seconds, the fuselage slammed into the ground, disintegrating the cabin and tossing trees and bodies across the top of the mountain to land on the other side. A minute after the initial impact, all motion stopped and the ground was eerily silent. The large jet had crashed in a remote section of the jungle, known as Buga.

# chapter two

# Tragedy on the Mountain

The crowds were buoyant at Alfonso International, until the revised 9:54 p.m. arrival time came and went. Dr. Carlos Reyes, a neurosurgeon at Cali's University Hospital and the father of Mauricio Reyes, a Michigan college student traveling home for Christmas, became concerned. Waiting with Dr. Reyes was his eldest son, Juan Carlos Reyes, an opthamologist in Cali who continued to press airline officials for answers to the delay. After several agonizing minutes, an official announced that the tower had lost contact with the plane. The crowd erupted into pandemonium.

When Juan saw an ambulance pull up outside the terminal, he ran towards it, pleading with them to let him go to the crash site. Inside there were eighteen paramedics and two physicians, and after further prodding they agreed to let Juan join the team. Leading the medical crew would be Dr. Laureano Quintero, a thirty-four-year-old bachelor renowned for his dedication and long hours in the trauma unit at Cali's University hospital.

Juan joined them for the forty-five-minute drive to the town of Buga, where the team found a group of local firemen who directed them up the rugged terrain. Leaving their ambulances on a path in the jungle, the team began to hike up the mountain on foot, in the dark, frigid night.

"If you see a man who looks like me, it's my brother," Juan Reyes said to the others.

Mauricio Reyes had been seated in the center of the airplane over the wing, beside another college student from the United States, Mercedes Ramirez, from Missouri. Mercedes was traveling with her mother, also named Mercedes, and her father, a teddy bear of a man who was originally from Colombia. The senior Mercedes was a woman with boundless energy, known to keep positive sayings posted inside her locker at work. She was the perfect balance for Mercedes's father, a quiet, sensitive man.

In the seats beside Mauricio in the very same row were Gonzalo Dussan, a copy technician from New Jersey, and Nancy, his companion of fourteen years. They were traveling with their two children, Michelle and Gonzalo Jr.

The 757 had vanished in the night, fully loaded with 155 passengers, six flight attendants, and two pilots. With the exception of the flight crew, most of the travelers were on their way to Cali for an extended vacation, to spend the Christmas holidays with family and loved ones. The passengers had been in a festive mood, in anticipation of the celebration ahead.

Just after eleven, the telephone rang in the home of Sylvia and Brett Bullard. Their eight-year-old son Nicholas was tucked into bed, excited about the Christmas holiday. In less than five days, Santa Claus would come.

"Hello?" Sylvia answered the phone.

It was her mother's friend, who said that she thought a plane had crashed, and that it could be the same plane that Sylvia's mother and father and sister had taken to Cali, to visit family members. Sylvia's heart sank. As her thoughts turned to her mother and father, then to her baby sister, Mercedes.

She hung up, powerless and filled with questions. She handled the news as her mother would, by praying. *Please God, please help me with whatever will come my way,* she prayed. Her mother had always been a spiritual woman, and had prepared her for this moment. She taught her daughters the importance of leaving a legacy in the way she helped others, but she always put her husband and daughters, Sylvia and Mercedes, first.

Sylvia then thought of her father. He had said once that his wish to God was that he would die in his homeland of Colombia. Her parents could not live without each other, they had said, and because of that they had wished for God to take them together, at the same time.

*They're all gone,* she thought, suddenly feeling like an orphan. In her heart she knew that they were dead, a thought that overwhelmed her. Sylvia was overtaken by loneliness, because although she had her husband and her son, they had not been a part of her past, only her present and future. She felt like a floater. It would be the longest night of her life.

# chapter three

# The Rescue

The search team trudged up the mountain. If there were to be any survivors, the plane would have to be found quickly, because after an impact with trees, the smoldering fire would spread fast. The seats, fabric, and windows could melt and disintegrate in seconds, leaving little time for evacuation.

The aluminum skin of the airplane, at one twentieth of an inch thick, could be penetrated within sixty seconds, creating a toxic inferno on the inside of the cabin. In previous crashes, passengers had been rendered unconscious from toxins in the smoke. If there were any survivors at all, they would need to get out of the fuselage within the first few minutes. Airplane crash sites could be unpredictable, fraught with hazardous substances such as jet fuel and carbon monoxide, that would deprive vital organs such as the brain, heart, and lungs of oxygen.

Mauricio's brother hiked the mountain for hours alongside the others. Mauricio was a business major at the University of Michigan, but had recently considered a change to medicine, to follow along in the footsteps of his brother and father. He was the baby of the family.

By seven the following morning, Juan Reyes and the others on the rescue team continued to search, discouraged that the missing airplane was nowhere in sight. At one point, they came upon a group of locals who pointed up the mountain, towards the area the airplane may have come to rest, so they moved quickly.

Juan Reyes stayed with the team, while one experienced paramedic, John Bueno, made the decision to separate from the group, following his own instincts over the mountain in another direction. The paramedic trekked alone against the rising sun without a compass or radio, looking out for leftist guerrillas and drug traffickers. After awhile he came upon a group of men, and was relieved to learn that they were just another team searching for the wreckage. Bueno continued to move towards the far side of the mountain, and twelve hours after the airplane went down, he stumbled upon a horrific scene.

The bodies were scattered in one area, in a circle about a hundred yards across. There were too many to count, and none were moving. The airplane had sheared trees all the way down, snapping them like twigs, creating a clear path in the thick forest. When the jet impacted with the ground, it catapulted pieces of fuselage, seats, luggage, and bodies across the top of the mountain ridge to the other side.

John Bueno shouted to a group of soldiers to radio for help, and then he stopped suddenly, his eyes resting on five survivors amidst the destruction. In one spot was Mauricio Reyes, nineteen, dazed and moaning, with blood and injuries on his face. Huddled beside him was Mercedes Ramirez, twenty-one. On the ground nearby there were three others clinging to life. Gonzalo Dussan, thirty-six, sat by his two children, six-year-old Michelle and thirteen-year-old Gonzalo Jr., who had all flown from their home in New Jersey.

Gonzalo Sr. could remember no warning during the flight, until he woke up on the ridge of the mountain. Everything was scattered around him: splintered trees, a mail pouch, pieces of luggage, and a teddy bear. Below them, there was a valley so dark that the mountains blocked the lights from towns on either side. Gonzalo knew that they had been in an accident. His daughter had blood on her face and was shivering from hypothermia. His son was bleeding from the impact. They waited there for hours on the frigid ground, the night air dense and black, the sky confusing. Were they in the United States or somewhere else? Strange sounds filtered through the forest.

\*  \*  \*

The paramedics rushed forward, beginning the process of stabilizing the survivors. One of them called for an army helicopter. The airplane had crashed into a mossy area, and the survivors had remained on the 12,000-foot mountain throughout the night, huddling together to fight the cold. Under normal circumstances, the valley was beautiful, lush and green with rolling hills in an assortment of colors. But on this night, the valley seemed surreal and chaotic.

Rescuers worked to stabilize Gonzalo's neck, which had suffered some sort of fracture. They were careful to make sure they didn't do further damage, and braced it until a helicopter could arrive. Mercedes had severe abdominal trauma and other injuries.

Rescuers worked on Michelle, a tiny girl with thick, black hair and big eyes. The survivors were losing blood and suffering from the cold, and would have to be rushed to the nearest hospital.

In the valley, the helicopter hovered, finding the wreckage quickly. But the winds had picked up, making it impossible to land. The rescue team made a decision to ease each survivor into a rectangular basket, which would be hoisted up into the sky to the chopper. One by one they went, transported to base camp for the long drive to the hospital in Cali.

Five passengers had survived the initial impact, and they all shared at least one thing in common. Remarkably, they had been seated next to one another in the same row, over the wing. Seat belts secured, they had prepared for a normal landing, but it was not until much later that they would understand the landing had been any-thing but normal, and that every passenger, including those within arms reach, just inches in front of their row and in the seats behind them, did not survive.

# chapter four

# The Call

The call comes in the middle of the night, invading my dream. It is just after one in the morning and the Dallas sky peering in from the bedroom window is black.

"We've had an accident," says the woman matter-of-factly.

Her voice is flat and unfamiliar. In seconds, I leap from the bed to the floor, and my heart fills with terror as I visualize every face in my family. In rapid frames, their smiles and voices pass through my head and I struggle to connect the only two words I heard. We, the caller had said, and accident. My stomach turns.

"What happened?" I ask.

"I'm calling from airline headquarters," the woman says. "You need to activate everyone on your team and report to the building where the Emergency Response Team will be stationed, as soon as possible."

In one moment I jolt from confusion to relief to sadness. My heart races. My family is safe, but the unthinkable has occurred. Four months earlier, I had completed training for the Emergency Response Team, a select group of individuals within the airline who would be faced with responding to an aircraft disaster in the unlikely event of a crash. There were more than five hundred employees on this team system-wide, and I was one of the newest.

I had participated in a two-day intensive training course designed to determine who would have the emotional and physical skills necessary to handle a major crisis. American had enjoyed a spotless record with few accidents and was firmly entrenched as one of the Big Six airlines in the nation. *It's highly unlikely you'll ever have to use this training*, the instructor had said.

"An airplane has gone down in a remote area of South America," the woman on the phone explains. "But we aren't sure of the exact location yet. The airplane is missing."

I process what follows in blurry fragments, but catch enough to understand that the plane had been filled with holiday travelers, many of them Americans on their way to visit relatives in Colombia. Nothing has been found—not the airplane, nor the black box, which will be the key that will unlock the mystery of why the plane disappeared.

I am aware that the black box is crafted of a resilient, fireproof material with a titanium outer casing. Inside is a container of microchips containing sixteen megabytes of memory within a spherical ball, the strongest shape against impact. The box contains a second layer of insulation crafted from a polymer-based material and would weigh about twenty-seven pounds, as much as a small dog. It is the best hope for a true record of any conversations that occur in the cockpit, and the last technical details from the aircraft.

I have seen a black box and know that they are easy for rescuers to identify, because of their bright orange color and white diagonal stripes. One side is etched with the words FLIGHT RECORDER DO NOT OPEN, and on the other, ENREGISTREUR DE VOL NE PAS OUVRIR.

"The area the aircraft is thought to be located in is a small stretch of mountain terrain known to be inhabited by leftist guerrillas," says the caller.

"Guerrillas?" My mind blurs. This doesn't seem real.

"Yes. Turn your television to CNN to get updates on the accident and tell your team to do the same. You need to plan on getting here as soon as possible to help with the initial activation. We can use you here in Dallas."

"Okay."

"And I know you're a new team leader, so it would be wise to quickly review your manual before calling your team. Assess their skills, then report back in to the command center with their data sheets. Anyone bilingual in Spanish will be a big asset. Also tell everyone to read the cultural guide for Latin America, the section in the manual outlining the cultural differences and religious practices. Some of them will be sent down to the crash site."

"When?"

"I don't have that information yet, but the Go-Team is on its way down on a special charter flight. The company has secured a toll-free number for the passengers' families and friends to call in on, and we'll be releasing it to the media. The chairman will hold a news conference first thing in the morning."

I had been taught that the Go-Team would consist of a core group of key airline officials, including the chairman and the director of the Emergency Response Team. They would most likely be be the first to arrive in Cali, and the first thing they'd do is hold a meeting with the general manager of the airport there, and immediately establish a command center. The Go-Team will also be charged with the task of contacting all officials in Cali to get the crash investigation rolling, coordinating activities at the hotel the airline will use and activating the emergency team's response. In every major incident, Go-Team members will work to assess the number of Emergency Response Team members needed for the crash activation, and will preassemble everything team members will need, from spending money to cell phones and pagers, down to the smallest details such as pens and paper for the command center. The Go-Team will also arrange for security, establish lines for phones and faxes, reserve hotel rooms and rental cars, and work with headquarters to relay information for updated news releases.

I wrap myself in a bathrobe and retrieve the Emergency Response Team manual from the top shelf of the closet in my brother's house, where I have been staying while in Dallas for meetings. I had spent nine years with the airline, moving swiftly up the corporate ladder, and now I had accepted a promotion that would entail a move from Florida to Dallas. I would oversee a sales territory for Sabre, the technical sister company to the airline that had developed the world's first airline reservation system. Instead of selling airline seats and marketing the airline, now I would be responsible for selling the technology behind the scenes to major corporations. In essence, still the same goal; getting companies to commit dollars and market share to our product. American had the best safety record in the industry, a major selling point for any airline, and one I had spent my entire career talking about. I had been recruited straight from college, and the sales team I met during my first week on the job consisted of high-caliber executives, men and women who had received years of specific sales training tailored to client management and presentation skills. I had been immediately enrolled in a sales training course and prepped for my initial assignment: a trip to Paris to introduce twenty corporate executives to American's new International service. What could be better? From the beginning, I was hooked.

But now, more than nine years have gone by and I find myself on the other end of a call I never could have imagined. It is December, 1995, and an airplane has been lost.

"Are there any survivors?" I ask. The question is met with silence. Adrenaline rushes through me, and my thoughts spiral, jumping to one step, then the next, thinking of the things I need to do. Airline manual, clothes, cell phone.

"It's too early to know," she says finally.

She hangs up without giving me her name, but I know what the next step has to be. I move upstairs, place the Emergency Response Team manual on the carpet in the landing, and sit in front of the open pages. Step one: contact all team members and prepare them for activation.

The file containing the individual data sheets of the Emergency Response Team members is thick and contains personal information on people I have never met. I spread them out on the floor in front of me and pick up the phone. I will wake them from slumber with a call that will change everything they have planned for the Christmas holidays. I sit in the darkness on the landing and realize that in one minute I will deliver the news that will thrust them into the center of the tornado.

I place the first call to my new boss, the vice president of sales, who will have to find a replacement to take over my duties as a sales manager for the next few days, weeks, or months. I have his home number in my computer, but it is late, so I dial his office and leave a voicemail, knowing that he will have no choice but to understand.

My previous manager, Sara Johnson, had recommended me for the Emergency Response Team and any manager following her would have to comply. The program had been sanctioned by the company chairman and had become an important part of the family-assistance process during activations, something that had become an increasingly significant issue. Although the program had been written about in newspapers after previous crashes, the details were foreign to most of the general public and to airline employees who had not been exposed to it.

"It would be a good experience for you," Johnson had said. "And it will look great on your resume."

I joined without question, never imagining that an accident would actually occur. Like most airline employees, I was fiercely loyal, with no intention of ever leaving. I had heard others use the phrase "I've got jet fuel in my blood," and after a year I knew what it meant. The airline industry has one of the lowest employee turnover rates in any business, and not because of the salaries. Although airline personnel are historically underpaid compared to their counterparts in other industries, they stay. They board airplanes whenever they wish, traveling on any given day to far corners of the world. They can fly free to visit their kids in college and their relatives can fly free, too, as well as anyone else they wish to give a ticket to. It did not take me long to become one of them, and after my first year, I found myself caught in the magical web, enraptured by the mystery of air travel and the benefits of working for an airline.

I had no reservations about the Emergency Response Team training program and was eager to attend. There were no papers to sign, no trying or wretched moments that one with an unformed, young heart could not handle. Just two days of emotionally charged crisis training where every response was examined under a microscope to determine who would be tough enough mentally, physically, and emotionally to respond to a major air disaster. Two days of *practice* for an emergency, where I had been required to think swiftly and provide instant answers to difficult questions: *Why do you want to be on a crisis response team? How do you think your life will change after being exposed to a major tragedy?* Two days of role-playing and crushing testimony from people who had experienced the tragedy of previous airplane crashes, along with stories that outlined the errors other airline Emergency Response Teams had made: one released the wrong emergency telephone number to the media after a crash, another informed a family about the death of their daughter with a message left on an answering machine, and yet another sent a FedEx package full of clothing from the wreckage to a man whose wife had died in the airplane crash, without any advance warning.

For the instructors, the most important task was to convince those of us willing to become part of the team that the job was more meaningful than any other assignment and not to be taken lightly. But in the comfort of the air-conditioned conference room, the possibility of standing amidst the wreckage of an air disaster seemed remote. Responding to an airplane crash would be a rare and adventurous experience, one that only a handful of people would ever realize. It would be a chance to help others, an opportunity to make an impact during a situation far beyond anyone's control.

On the last day of training, each of us had been told to go home and pack a suitcase immediately, one that would be stuffed with clothes that would remain tucked inside like a bounty for years, until the dreaded event occurred. The suitcase would be plucked from the back of a closet, dusted off, and shoved in the trunk of the car after we were activated, with the idea being that there would be one less thing to think about. The suitcase was mandatory. If no incident ever occurred, the payoff of joining the team would be far greater than the two-day investment in the training class and the twenty minutes involved in packing a suitcase.

But now, reality has struck. I am anxious to delve into whatever I will be required to do, and ready to go to Cali, if I have to.

# chapter five

# The Team

The cultural guide for Colombia is a single page of information. I scan it briefly, jotting notes in a small spiral notebook. Race, religion, funeral arrangements. Unique cultural and religious beliefs. If at all possible, an Emergency Response Team member should be of the same race and religious affiliation as the family he or she is assigned to, so that the family will feel more comfortable in their dealings with our staff.

It's a sensitive time and in Colombia the cultural differences are vast. Colombian households are patriarchal and rely heavily on the male head of the house to conduct the communication for the family, especially in times of great importance, such as this one. For that reason, a male Emergency Response Team contact would be best suited for the primary interactions with a family.

I search through my documents and place the team members with Hispanic-sounding names at the top of the stack. Every team will have twenty to thirty team members, some that are bilingual and some that are not. I have several team members based in Miami, and others who are scattered in various parts of the southern United States.

When an airplane crash occurs, there are five major tasks the members of an Emergency Response Team are asked to perform, one of which is a family assignment. When a team member is assigned to a victim's family, he or she does everything within their power to make sure that the family is accommodated and their needs are met. The assignment is emotionally taxing and may include buying groceries, getting a car repaired, seeing to it that the family's house and pets are taken care of while they're at the crash site, assisting with funeral preparation, and attending the funeral itself.

Other tasks that team members perform include placing the initial notification call to the families to tell them that their loved ones were on the ill-fated airplane, arranging for the victim's families to get to the crash location, and flying to the location of the crash site.

Normally, tasks during a crash activation are assigned based on each team member's individual skill set and personality type, which is determined in advance by their assigned team leader. After an individual completes the two-day training program, he or she is assigned to work under a leader in a specific geographic region. This leader will follow up the training with an introductory phone call and attempt to evaluate the individual's abilities and knowledge by phone to begin the coding process that will remain on file.

Is a new member of the team bilingual? If so, it's noted in his or her file. Candidates who speak multiple languages are vital after a crash because there are numerous nationalities represented on any given airplane and some of the initial notification calls are placed to family members overseas. Has a team member been rated as having strong administrative skills yet weaker interpersonal skills? The information is noted in the team member's file and this specific personality type would be assigned a task such as booking air reservations for families to get to the crash site versus a face-to-face assignment with a family.

Individual team members reside all over the world, so it's likely that a team leader will not have met his or her team members prior to an activation. This means the team leader must do the best job possible in evaluating skills based on the application on file, or from a brief telephone conversation with the new team member.

The team leader is someone who has been identified as having exceptional leadership skills and is usually someone who has been exposed to at least one crash activation. I am an exception, only because I have been asked to take over the team of an older, seasoned executive who has retired from the company. I've inherited a list of thirty or so Emergency Response Team members, all of whom have been through the required training program and some who have even worked previous crash activations.

*　*　*

It's 2:00 A.M., just five hours after the crash, when my first team member is startled from sleep. His profile tells me he's a mid-level manager in finance who has worked a previous activation. His name is Hector, he's from somewhere in Latin America, and he now lives in Miami with his wife and two children. His passport is current and he speaks English, Spanish, and some French. I deliver the news as it has been delivered to me, and he reacts calmly.

"Are you willing to travel to Cali?" I ask.

"Sign me up," he says without hesitation. His only question is what level activation this will be.

"Level one," I reply.

Airplane crashes, or "incidents," as we have been told to refer to them, have been defined by the company into three distinct categories—Levels 1, 2, and 3. Level 1 refers to any event involving a company plane where there have been major, life-threatening injuries and severe aircraft damage. In a Level 1 incident, there are fatalities. Emergency Response Team personnel are activated to the scene of the crash and are assigned to the victim's families. Level 1 incidents involve fire, smoke, and major aircraft damage combined with an influx of calls from the public due to extensive media coverage and controversy. In a

Level 1 accident, the cause of the crash may not be determined for years, due to the various agencies involved and complex investigation procedures.

Level 2 incidents are less severe and are usually the result of harsh turbulence or emergency landings. This type of incident is defined as any event where there are minor injuries that are not considered life threatening. If there are injuries involving a hospitalization, Emergency Response Team members are activated to work with the passengers and their families. If there are no injuries at all, it may not be necessary for the team to be activated. The least severe type of aircraft incident is categorized as a Level 3, an event with minimal aircraft damage and no reported injuries.

I ask Hector if he has any additional questions and advise him to remain on standby with his packed suitcase until his assignment has been made. I am 90 percent certain he'll go to the crash site, but the command-center officials doling out assignments will make that determination. In the next hour, officials in Dallas will weigh the severity of the crash against the skill set available within the system of team members we've been able to confirm for activation. The goal will be to get as many Spanish-speaking team members as possible to the crash location, victim's families, and reservation call center, without taxing the corporate system and crumbling the day-to-day operations of the airline. Although many of the candidates that meet the criteria will reside in Miami, if all the Emergency Response Team candidates from Miami were utilized, the daily airline operation in Miami could suffer. Activating a response team is a methodical, organized process that the airline has carefully planned.

Like the other airline employees I encountered in the training program, my team varies in personality and profile. Black, white, Hispanic. Older, younger, and everywhere in-between. Across the world, there are more than twenty team leaders like myself placing the initial kickoff call and more than five hundred team members from various countries. More than two hundred will be activated for this specific crash, most from the United States and Latin America. The team members will consist of nonmanagement employees such as baggage handlers, flight attendants, and ticket agents, as well as executives from sales, accounting, and other management-related positions.

I hang up with Hector and prepare to dial my next team member, finding it ironic that although I am the leader of my team, most have attended training long before I did and most have been through prior activations. They will be spread out all over the system performing various assignments during this activation and it's likely I'll never meet most of them. My team will be leading me.

* * *

In the stark conference room where Emergency Response Team training was held, the mood had been somber and the sessions filled with nervous laughter. The instructor, Jane Crowley, was an attractive brunette with the opportunity of a lifetime—to develop a crisis-management program that had already become the gold standard for other airlines in the industry. A program director for the largest airline in the United States, she carried a hefty responsibility. If a crash occurred, all eyes would be watching, including the public, the media, and the governing bodies of aviation. During an investigation, the airline would be examined under a microscope.

On day one, we were taught about specific airline procedures and the basics of a crash, beginning with the second an airplane has been disabled. Types of accidents, forensic terms, victim identification, and the emotional aftermath of a crash were presented in lessons, videos, and role-plays. The candidates seated around the conference table had one thing in common—we were all there to be assessed, and if we did not meet the criteria necessary to be on the team, our name would be crossed from the list. The instructor was clear about this point, but presented it in a nonthreatening manner, in a way that made it seem as if it would be all right if you were selected and all right even if you weren't. Either way, we were told, we were to feel proud for volunteering for such a difficult mission.

The first exercise entailed watching a videotaped testimony from a flight attendant who had survived a terrible crash in which several passengers died. It was a crash that had involved another airline, and the exercise was designed to prepare everyone emotionally for the effects of a crash. As the tape rolled, the attendant explained how she had just finished serving the meal in the coach cabin when the airplane started to jolt. Moments later, she found herself dangling from a seatbelt in midair, with two choices. She could wait for help to arrive amidst the chaos around her, or she could release herself and fall several feet to the hard ground below and then struggle to get out of the wreckage. Either way, she decided, she would be injured, but if she did nothing she might not escape.

The attendant recalled how she fumbled for the metal clasp and worked on it until she dropped to the ground. In minutes, she was scrambling out of the wreckage and away from a crash in which several lives were lost. At the end of the video, we were all left with the same feeling. It had been the flight attendant's quick decision that meant the difference between life and death. Instead of *waiting* for a rescue, she had decided that she would *survive*.

The television monitor illuminated the dark conference room. The air turned frigid and the class fidgeted in silence. The instructor turned the video off and I felt strangely suspended in purgatory between what was and what will be. Across the table, a manager from the accounting department swiveled in his chair in a constant back-and-forth motion, arms crossed over his chest like a shield. Beside him, a ticket agent from New York watched the monitor in anticipation, chewing on the end of a pencil until it was frayed and splintered. I knew from the introductions that some who had signed up for the Emergency Response Team program had the same motivation as I did. They had never turned from an open door, and were curious to walk through it. Others, like the baggage handler with two children, were hesitant about the open door yet they chose the assignment anyway and ignored the warning bells. Why? My guess is because the door had been cracked open and there was no turning back.

Within seconds, a girl broke down, her sobs filling the room. A knot formed in the center of my throat. Will she be sent home? I wondered and watched the instructor anxiously as she reached for a tissue box on the table and handed one to the girl, offering a reassuring smile.

Emotions were encouraged, but meeting the needs of the families we will work with during an activation would take precedence. It would mean that there could be no *victim identification syndrome*, no weeping, or becoming too close to the victim, identifying with his or her pain to the point where the job becomes difficult to perform. All the emotions we had allowed ourselves to feel would have to be bottled and put on a shelf. Emotions were nothing more than baggage, and if we carried the baggage along with us, everyone we touched would be affected, especially those we were trying to help.

"It is a job that *isn't for everyone*," the instructor said.

After the end of day one, I closed my spiral-bound notebook, mentally exhausted. On the cardboard cover, I drew a small suitcase and wrote the words "check it" beneath it. Above all else, I decided, I would strive to keep my emotions in check. If I felt sadness or despair, I would check it into my mental luggage and visualize throwing the bag on a conveyor belt that would take it away until it disappeared behind the black rubber mats into the back of the terminal. I would check my emotions to keep my emotions in check.

*  *  *

In Dallas, I sit by the phone with the profiles of my team members, CNN flickers in the darkness. The house is silent, except for the muted voices of the reporters who recount the tragedy of a downed aircraft. It's the lead story and every news channel has coverage, although there are no reports from the crash site yet.

The reporters say that the weather was clear in Cali and temperatures were normal. I know from my training that many passengers survive the majority of plane crashes if rescue crews can get there in time, and that the first sixty seconds of evacuation count the most. The clock on the wall ticks loudly, reminding me that it has been more than six hours since the airplane went down.

I pick up the telephone and exhale deeply. The first call was a breeze, so I continue to dial until twenty-five team members have been contacted, all roused from their sleep and surprised by the news. Most everyone has questions I cannot answer. Only one declines to be activated due to the Christmas holidays, so I delete him from the list. It's okay to say no, but few ever do. After everyone on my team has been contacted, I move to the guest room and search the closet for a duffle bag, a suitcase, or anything my brother might have that I could pack full of clothes. I had been in transition from one state to the other after accepting the new job, but even without the excuse of a move, I still wouldn't have packed the suitcase. The training had ended four months ago, and packing an activation suitcase seemed as if it would invite a tragedy, so I hadn't done it.

After stuffing a few shirts, sweaters, and pants into an abandoned nylon bag, I move to the damp garage and place it in the trunk of my rental car. I have chosen a pair of jeans, khakis, and a few corporate-looking blouses, along with a bottle of water and a package of batteries for flashlights or radios. I move back into the house and scan the manual again to make sure I'm not missing anything. Some of the team members will need current passports, so I make a note to ask about the emergency passport forms that will be submitted to the State Department. The airline's contact in

Washington will have the passports issued within one day, although most everyone should already have one since a passport is a requirement to be on the team.

I dress without showering and prepare for the short drive toward the Dallas airport where the primary command center has been established in a building near airline headquarters. I wake my brother before I leave to tell him what's going on, and he turns on the local news channel just in time to catch the camera crew standing in front of American Airlines's headquarters. We watch the coverage for a while, but there is nothing more than I have already been told.

"Are you ready for this?" he asks.

"As ready as I can be."

He gives me a hug.

At four in the morning, the streets that wind through my brother's north Dallas suburb are dark and quiet. Some houses are lit inside, revealing the shadows of early risers preparing for the long workday ahead. A woman in a housecoat two blocks down walks a small dog, the kind my grandfather refers to as mop dogs. *Good for nothing*, he would say. It pees on the tire of a car parked in the street and barks incessantly when I pass by. At the traffic light leading to the main road, there are dozens of businesses in strip malls, identical to the ones in Florida and every other city across America. *Starbucks, Target, Kinko's*. I long for a town without the conveniences of any of them, a town with character, where I'd have to search for an hour before finding a place with Internet access. A small, unknown village like the one in Vermont where my father's brother lives, with one general store that serves also as the post office, and where your cell phone blinks "out of service" the minute you enter city limits.

I pull away from the light towards the highway, passing a red-brick two-story identical to my brother's and most of the homes in this neighborhood. A light flickers just inside the bay window in the den. I wonder if someone else has awaken to the news I am now a part of.

All across America, they will turn on their coffee makers and televisions and get dressed for work while watching the news reports of the plane crash. Ordinarily it would be just another plane and just another crash, soon forgotten. But this morning when the world woke up it would be just four days before Christmas, and Christmas had a way of changing hearts. The news would be met with sadness, tears, and visions of a crash site filled with Christmas presents and wishes that will never be fulfilled.

By 4:15 I'm on the highway, moving along at a good pace on the toll road that runs through Dallas, connecting massive concrete interstates and overpasses. I pass the Galleria mall, and see the impressive display of lights and the spectacular Christmas tree above Saks Fifth Avenue. At the tollbooth, I roll down my window and pass coins to a black man wearing a Santa Claus cap, and the chill of the wind gusts through my window.

Although it was bound to happen, the prospect of a crash had never entered my mind, and now I feel only adrenaline at what lies ahead, not dread. I think about the others on the team and their motives for joining. It is the one thing that cannot be ascertained over the phone during a brief conversation in the night. *What would make someone want to participate in a tragedy?*

I turn the car radio to an all-news station and the reports are the same as CNN. The airplane has come to rest in a mountainous section of the forest, amidst dangerous terrain. It is thought that the plane can only be reached by helicopter, followed by a treacherous hike up the mountain. There are jaguars, snakes, and poisonous spiders. The survivors, if there are any, will be exposed to intolerable conditions in a dense jungle. The thought passes through me that at this exact moment, someone else is trapped in the wreckage of an airplane in a jungle more than a thousand miles away. I am here and they are there, but we are connected by fate. I imagine them cold, scared, and fighting to live. *Please hang on*, I say. *Please, just wait for someone to find you.*

# chapter six

# Initial Notification

I follow the winding roads leading through the Dallas airport complex until I find the massive concrete building that houses the initial activation center. The lot closest to the front entrance is crowded with hundreds of cars belonging to reservation employees who are here working their normal shift. Emergency Response Team members will stream in throughout the night, as they receive word of the crash, to assist with the telephones and the flood of incoming calls. Although incoming callers won't be given any information, to maintain security, the Emergency Response Team will log their names and numbers into the airline computer system for follow-up.

I park the car and slide my ID badge through a reader to gain entry to the building. Inside, I traverse the halls, following several crude handwritten signs affixed to the walls with masking tape up one flight of stairs, around corners, and down another long hallway. Christmas stockings hang from the walls of cubicles, some stuffed with candy and gifts. Leftover brownies grow stale on a desk, beside pictures from an office party. I come to a heavy door with a sign on it that tells me it's the activation center for the Emergency Response Team, and I knock twice. The door opens and I am immediately ushered into an explosion of activity.

The room is vast and filled with seventy or more airline employees engrossed in various tasks. One of them hands me a stack of file folders and instructs me to find an empty phone in a line of cubicles. Another one checks my identification.

"The airplane hasn't been found yet," he tells me. "Don't give any information out to the callers except for what's on this bulletin." He gives me a sheet of paper with a typewritten update. "Check the bulletin board hourly for updates, and if there is a question you can't answer, tell them that we will contact them again later when we know more."

He hands me a small green sticker with the Emergency Response Team logo.

"Affix this to the front of your identification badge. It will let everyone know you've been activated. Oh, and you'll need to contact the medical department to arrange all your shots."

"Shots?"

"You can't go to Latin America without vaccinations."

My heart races. I peel off the adhesive backing and press the sticker onto the front of my ID badge. I find for an empty desk and set up shop in the cubicle closest to the wall, preparing for the first step in the activation process.

Step one will be to make the initial notification call to the emergency contact listed in each passenger's flight records. I have heard that it's one of the most difficult and emotional tasks one can perform during a crash activation, because you are establishing contact with a passenger's family member, and it's likely to be the first time they've heard of the crash.

In the cubicle neighboring mine, a Hispanic girl in her twenties converses in Spanish with a victim's family member. In the cubicle beyond her, a man feeds documents through a paper shredder that hums each time it devours one, before regurgitating the remains into a clear plastic receptacle. In the cubicle adjacent to mine, I am stunned to see Liz Fleming, a former manager who I could go a lifetime without ever seeing again. Two years before, she had taken over our sales team and quickly earned a reputation for weekly tirades that would ultimately result in one of my colleagues being fired. Our close team of sales managers dwindled during the time she was there. I barely escaped her wrath.

When I finally left that job to take a promotion in another department, I had hoped I would never see Liz again. Liz glances up from the cubicle where she is working and sees me at once. I look away but it's too late. In seconds she's heading straight towards me.

"Tammyyyyy, how *are* you?" She throws her arms around me and squeezes so hard it feels like my ribs have been crushed.

"I'm fine, thanks. Are you on the Emergency Response Team?"

"Oh yes. Isn't it terrible? They haven't found the plane yet." Her voice is soft, and I can see from the red around her eyes that she's been crying. She seems vulnerable, not at all like the Liz I once knew.

"I can't believe this has happened," she sniffs. "Brace yourself for the initial notification calls. They're really tough."

She is gone as quickly as she came. Across the hall, a high-ranking vice president who reports directly to the CEO mingles with the lower-level employees who work the phones. His normally confident face is drawn, and dark circles have formed beneath both eyes. The tragedy has neutralized rank and profile.

I lower myself into the stiff gray chair to contemplate the files containing the lives I will forever alter. The initial notification call is the first task performed by the Emergency Response Team after a crash. It the assignment that the majority of team members volunteer for, because they believe that it will provide more emotional distance than the other tasks. The call is often met with a family member in denial, but it's a phone call, not a face-to-face visit. In training, we were taught that neutralizing the traumatic aftereffects of an air disaster begins with that very first call to the emergency contact in the reservation record. If no emergency contact has been given, the process is delayed, because the team will have to identify a valid, primary contact based on the list of people who have called in to inquire about that specific passenger.

The call is vital because it sets in motion the process of events that will lead the person on the other end of the line to his or her missing relative or loved one. If the line is busy or the number is outdated, this one missing detail can cause the family to lose crucial seconds with a loved one who may have been transported to a hospital. Once the call has been successfully completed, the next step is to arrange physical transportation for the family members to the crash site, hospital, morgue, or wherever their loved one is located.

Each file folder is a dichotomy in itself. Cheery yellow cardstock, brightly colored, with the victim's last name followed by the first scrawled in despondent black marker on the tab. The letters are thick and careless and veer off the folders as if the author had been distracted. But the handwriting is elegant and distinct like the kind possessed by one who has been schooled in architecture.

The file folders seem odd to me. I trace my hand over the smooth cover of the one on top, knowing that its thin contents bear heavy burdens. The data inside can't possibly depict the details of a full life hallmarked with promotions, family, babies, marriage, hurts, dreams, and trips to foreign lands. I cautiously open the first file. The name Alan Prill is typed at the top of a computer printout containing his itinerary, which is the only thing inside. One thin piece of paper. That's all there is. I scan it quickly, then place it back into the empty file folder.

I pick up the telephone and prepare to deliver a heavy heart to Alan's twenty-three year-old daughter, Jennifer. The stack of file folders suddenly seems heavy.

"Hello, is Jennifer there?"

"Yes…this is Jennifer." Her voice is broken, and I can tell she's been crying.

*She has already heard the news.* I introduce myself and a sob escapes her throat. She knows that what comes next is a confirmation that the nightmare is real.

"Do you have a family member there with you?" I ask gently.

Delivering the news of an airplane crash could cause a passenger's family member to go into shock, which is why it's imperative to make certain someone else is in the house with them. I wait patiently until I can hear another voice in the background.

"Jennifer, your father was on our flight that went down last night in Colombia, Flight 965 from Miami." I deliver the news swiftly then repeat myself once more. "We have confirmed that he was on the airplane last night, but that's all I know at this time. I'm sorry."

The phone is silent. As I await her reply, I think of how I have spent a lifetime longing for my own father, wanting desperately to understand someone I will never know. My mind goes back to when I was seven, to the day he killed himself in the apartment. Did he say something to me before he did it? Was I there? Did I block everything out? Did I try to talk him out of it? Tragedy plays tricks on you, twisting your memory until you aren't really sure if it's real or something your mind has fabricated to shelter you from the truth. I have tried many times over the years to understand why it happened, seeking counselors, experts in suicide, and in one desperate moment I'd never admit to anyone, a psychic. Throughout my life I have been haunted by the questions, yet the answers will never be revealed. Tragedy is not tidy. It comes with an impossible lack of control, and creates a void so large that you must learn to accept it or be swallowed by it. I push the thought away.

"Jennifer?" I ask. "Are you there?"

"No, I spoke with him. It's not true! I heard it on the news..."

*No. It's not true. I heard it on the news...* I wait several seconds, processing my reply.

Slowly, I confirm the information again, but this time with a softer voice, though I know it can make no difference. When I think that she has really understood, or at least that I've done my job, I give her our toll-free emergency family number in case she needs any further information. I hang up the phone without remembering how our conversation ended or if we even said good-bye and I move Jennifer to the bottom of the pile, preparing to dial the next family.

This family has a Spanish surname and one emergency contact noted in their passenger record. The file contains their names, Marsha and Lawrence, and from the calls we have received it looks as if they had been traveling to Latin America to visit an elderly mother. The male passenger is in his fifties, with a family originally from Latin America. The female passenger is his wife, also in her fifties, with family residing in New England. The passenger record notes that a son called in immediately after news reports of the crash, but in the chaos he did not leave his number. I dial the emergency-contact number the passengers had given the agent at the airport, but it rings busy. I dial the number again and it still rings busy. I move to the next file, read through it, and wait ten minutes. I try the first number once more, but again it rings busy. I am certain the contact is on the phone in a frantic attempt to learn more about the whereabouts of his family, but he does not have call waiting, so his file goes to the bottom of the pile. The next family must be called.

After several continuous hours on the phone delivering bad news to families, an executive in a crumpled suit enters the room, searches for an empty chair, and climbs onto it. He announces his name, which I cannot hear above the voices, and his title, which is a high-level manager in passenger sales, the department that sells and markets the airline to corporations. Passenger sales is one of the most sought-after departments in the company, the same department I was hired in. Though employees usually rise through the ranks to get there, even the lowest-level passenger-sales managers have the authority to give free airline tickets to corporate clients, individuals, or charities. Another benefit is the steady supply of upgrades and frequent-flyer-club memberships the managers have at their disposal, along with the celebrity golf tournaments and dinners with CEOs. Most work from home and have the luxury of golfing with clients and lunching with friends in the travel industry.

The executive on the chair shouts across the room, waiting until the flurry of activity grinds to a halt. "Excuse me!" he says, "Colombian soldiers located parts of the wreckage around 6:30 this morning. The passengers were found just after nine, and although it's too early to speculate on numbers, survivors *have* been found in the wreckage."

The room erupts. The girl working beside me throws her arms around my neck and squeezes hard, bouncing up and down. The file folder in my hand crumples, and when she pulls back, her face is streaked with tears and mascara.

"Can we please quiet down?" The man clears his throat.

"The plane crashed about two hundred feet from the top of a mountain in an area called Buga. We don't know how many survivors there are at this point, and it's a long hard trip up and down the mountain, accessible only on foot. The survivors had to be carried down the mountain because it was far too windy at the crash site for the helicopter to land and pull them out. The conditions on the mountain are extreme, so let's all be cautiously optimistic, and as always, do not talk to the press. Please refer all press questions to the corporate communications desk. There's also a report or maybe a rumor," he adds, "that a young man has hired a helicopter to search the crash site for his missing brother. This is likely to cause an influx of calls and questions, and you all need to understand what's happening. Once again, please make sure you do not comment on it. Forward all calls of that nature to corporate communications."

"Do we know who the survivors are?" the question comes from the front of the room.

"I have information on one of them," the man responds. "Mercedes Ramirez, a white female, twenty-one years of age. She's an American college student from Northwest Missouri State University. She's been transported to the hospital with severe injuries and is currently listed in critical condition. Let's all pray she pulls through."

At nine P.M., I am back on the highway again, driving back to my brother's house after fifteen hours of calling passengers' families. I have not slept, but I am not tired. The adrenaline moves through me and my mind races from one thought to the next until so many thoughts have cluttered the corners of my brain. I've been asked to fly to the crash site and I am ready to go. I dial my husband at our home in Florida and we talk for the first time since the accident. Although there are a thousand miles between us, his voice is a familiar comfort and it is in this moment that I realize I have been like a turbulent wave, crashing against the shore of his life. We were married so young, and I have yet to resolve things that occurred in the dawn of my life, things that everyone has to face at one time or another in order to become whole. He has been patient with me, but our future remains uncertain.

"How was it?" he asks. "Are you all right?"

I tell him about the command center, about the families I called.

"What was it like?" he asks.

"It was no big deal."

The line is silent. I did not expect it to be difficult, because I had no expectations at all. I had jumped in without a thought, like I did with most things, like I had with my marriage and everything else. *I was born to do this job*, I thought. *I feel fine.*

"Well I'm here if you need me," he says quietly.

For a moment I remember the suitcase in the trunk and think of how different things would be if I boarded a flight to Tampa instead and surprised him at the front door of our home. I am at a crossroads in every way, but there is no turning back. I have a sense that a new door is open and I'm halfway through it, a sense that most people who are at the sunset of one thing and sunrise of another feel, but cannot pinpoint.

"When will you be home?" he asks, but it is a question I cannot answer.

"I have no idea. I'll call you from Colombia."

* * *

When I arrive back at my brother's house, I shower for the first time in two days and step into a pair of sweats. I'm excited, detached, and ready to board the airplane right away. The adrenaline makes sleep impossible, so I recline in the leather chair in the middle of the living room and stare at the chunks of plaster on the ceiling. My mind races, and I check the clock. The command center had been loud, but the house is so still it's deafening. I would rather be back in the fray.

It's been several hours and I've not shed one tear, a thought that gives me satisfaction. I have excelled at one thing in my life, pushing away the pain. Some take satisfaction in being the kind of person who *feels*, but a friend once told me I was like the tin man in the Wizard of Oz, without a heart. I close my eyes and think about this. I know that I have one, but it turned to stone long ago, when I was a child who realized that my father would never be coming back. In my mind, he didn't think I was important enough, or he would have been with me, and each time I witnessed my friends doing things after school with their fathers, I was reminded of it. I think of the people who have lost their fathers in the plane crash.

It was easier than I had imagined, calling all those people, even when they reacted with hysterics and denial. I keep the television muted and watch the same footage on CNN over and over, observing the victim's family members caught on camera in airports across the globe. They scramble to get to the crash site as if doing so will change what has happened. Many have cellulars pinned to their ears, no doubt in hopes of receiving good news. I move to the floor, close to the screen. The camera is fixed on a young girl wearing jeans and an oversized men's shirt that looks as if she has thrown it on at the last minute. Her hair is flaxen and piled on top of her head in a knot. She is beautiful and frightened and I can't help but wonder if it's Jennifer, the girl I had phoned just hours earlier. The CNN reporter outlines the crash location. *Mountainous terrain known for guerrilla activity. No reported survivors.* I want to jump through the television and grab the reporter by the neck.

"There is a survivor!" I say.

The camera scans the crowded airport before fixing on the girl again. It follows her worried expression while she dials the cell phone. I rise from the carpet and scan the walls of the living room, lightheaded. When I start for the bedroom, I turn back one more time and the girl is still there, staring vacantly at the camera. This time, she is answering the questions of a relentless interviewer. I reach for the remote and turn up the volume. "I just want to find my father," she says steadily, and my stomach tightens. It is such a simple request.

# chapter seven

# The Search Continues

The headline jumps out from the holiday edition of *USA Today*: "Miracle at jet crash site." The Red Cross in Cali has reported eight people taken from the wreckage alive, but a firefighter puts the number at five. Rescue officials hope to find more survivors in the wreckage in the next few days.

News reports offer several different speculations on the cause of the crash. One reporter interviews an aviation expert, who prematurely theorizes that it could have been pilot error, and another station reports that a farmer on the mountain saw an explosion prior to the impact. Another expert points to the lack of sufficient navigational systems in Colombia or sabotage by guerrillas, but the truth is, no one really knows.

For the next three days, I dress casually in jeans and a sweatshirt and drive back and forth to the primary activation center in Dallas, making calls to families, fielding inbound questions from concerned loved ones, and helping the crash operation move along as smoothly as possible. It is now evident that more than a hundred passengers have died, names on a passenger list that do not seem real.

On Christmas morning, I drive to the airport to board the flight that will take me to Miami and then Cali. For the first time I find myself thinking of the what-ifs, as if anything could change what has happened. What if Jennifer's father had gotten the flu and had decided to stay home for another week? What if the people in Latin America at the small division of his company changed the meeting date, deciding it was too close to the Christmas holiday?

I pull off the highway onto the long road leading to the Dallas Fort Worth airport terminal, which is dominated by the three major U.S. carriers, American, Delta, and United.

As I move through security, I feel butterflies gathering in my stomach, not at the thought of the tasks I'll perform, but at the excitement of entering the unknown. I have traveled the world and negotiated Latin America before, but I am aware now that even if I do not leave my hotel, this trip will be unlike any other.

It is not danger I feel. I have taken previous trips to the third world, and on one particular trip I flew to Guatemala after volunteering for the delicate assignment of transporting a severely deformed baby back to her family. She had undergone maxofacial surgery in the United States and a charitable organization I was involved with had arranged for her return. But when I landed in the dingy Guatemalan airport terminal at midnight, I had felt a shiver of fear. The terminal was submerged in total darkness from an apparent power outage, or something else. A man with a machine gun shuttled all of us through a long hallway, where there were other men with machine guns. The infant was cradled in my arms, rolled up inside a pink blanket and I could not stop thinking of the controversy and rumors about foreigners stealing babies from Latin America to sell on the black market. It was considered unsafe for Americans to travel to the region, yet there I was at midnight, a white woman carrying a Latin baby. Despite my ignorance, I returned safely, wanting to do it all over again.

At Dallas airport, I continue through the crowd and present my ERT identification badge to the agent directing traffic at the first-class counter at American. The line is long, secured by two strands of red velvet rope leading to the ticket agents. Passengers waiting are ushered to the ticket counter on a long, red carpet, like celebrities at an awards show.

"You're activated for the Emergency Response Team?" the agent asks. I nod in confirmation and her brows pop high above her spectacles.

The Emergency Response Team has been a mysterious entity for years, a program that most people in the company find intriguing. Their reactions astonish me since it is the innate nature of airline people to be jaded, because of the things they've experienced. Talk to any airline employee and they'll relate fascinating stories about the world. They know the currency in Tonga and the unique way the rain smells at Machu Picchu. They've negotiated with Indians in Otavalo and watched the mystifying fog envelop Loch Walensee in Switzerland. They know that taxis have sirens in Singapore and that in Romania you had better not show affection to a dog, because dogs are considered unclean, not part of the family like in America.

To an airline employee, the world is free, and the baggage handlers and ticket agents have seen places most other passengers have never been. Airline employees are world-weary, and if that is not enough, they have seen every display of human weakness and emotion. They respond calmly to irate passengers, they've witnessed heart attacks in airport terminals, and they have been exposed to the kindness of strangers. In any single day, the airport is a self-contained world.

"Do they know why it happened yet?" asks the ticket agent, leaning in.

Suddenly I am an expert, though I know nothing more than anyone else.

"No, too early," I reply.

She leans closer and whispers in my ear. "I think it was a bomb, personally. There's all that drug stuff going on down there and there was a drug-cartel guy on the plane. Did you know that?"

"No, I didn't."

There have been more than forty-five incidents involving bombs aboard various airlines and airplanes that have resulted in the deaths of passengers and crew. But I have heard nothing about a bomb involved with this one.

"That's what I just heard anyways," she said. "You checking anything?"

"No."

She eyes my one piece of luggage and ushers me to the front of the line where an agent behind the desk issues me a boarding card in the exit row.

When an airplane goes down, it creates a ripple effect that travels across the globe. In the media, rumors abound and often it is months before the actual cause of the crash is known. Sometimes, the cause remains a mystery, but when news of a crash hits, the emotional impact runs deep and the story travels thousands of miles to the crisis workers, then the victim's families, then down-line to friends and distant relatives. As representatives of the airline, the employees are likely to feel some sense of ownership for the loss, because in every fatal crash, unlike accidents that occur in other industries, the airline loses its own people.

The airplane I'll be taking from Dallas is a 757, the same model aircraft that hit the mountain five days ago. I board behind a long line of passengers and settle into my row, stuffing the duffle bag under the seat in front of me. When I lean back in the seat, my left arm is throbbing, and I press my palm against it to quell the pain. The day prior, I had received a mandatory series of shots for the trip. Every team member traveling to the crash site would be vaccinated against malaria, hepatitis, and other deadly diseases that can be easily contracted in third-world countries through contact with contaminated food, water, or humans. The entire series of shots had taken less than ten minutes, and the nurse at company headquarters had been efficient and knowledgeable. She left me with a thick packet of information on the various diseases and their symptoms, but with all the reading material I already had for the journey, I left it behind.

I search for the button on my armrest and press it to recline, placing the crisis-team manual inside a large notebook so that no one can see what I'm reading. Initially, I scan the page containing the hierarchy of events surrounding a crash activation and then the organizational chart of the people involved. Specific roles are outlined, and I read mine to make sure I'm equipped to meet their expectations. We have one stop to make in Miami, but when we touch down in Cali I'll be responsible for getting myself to the airline command center. Once there, I and the other team members who arrive from various cities and states will receive our Go-Kits, the preassembled communication packages containing pagers, cell phones, and a stipend of local currency.

The customs and culture in Cali will differ from my own, and my team will need to be aware of them. In Latin America, the economy is generally depressed, but Colombia is rich in diversity with a population working in crude oil, coal, coffee, and cut flowers, the principal exports. For years, Americans and other foreigners have been kidnapped, and there is a proliferation of trafficking women and children for sex. Other problems include the killing of prostitutes and street children and the mysterious murders of those considered socially undesirable. Colombia is a country with a strong religious faith based in Catholicism, although even religious leaders have been assassinated. The inhabitants of Colombia live in a mix of neighborhoods and religious communities and include a surprisingly significant population of Mennonites, who can be spotted navigating carts and horse-drawn buggies along country roads. The Mennonites settled here from various parts of the United States years before, in desire of a quiet, isolated place where they could raise their families according to their own customs.

At the command center in Cali, staff members will work in Sabre, the airlines' reservation system, to communicate with the staff in the United States. Sabre has its own language, an intricate series of complex characters that every employee must learn. Computers will be used to document information on the passengers on a daily basis and update Emergency Response Team records. The flight records of the airplane have already been seized and locked to prevent viewing by any outside parties, which is standard procedure after a crash. The passenger name list has been pulled and distributed to aviation authorities, and our Go-Team has created special passwords for the crisis task force to use. The flight number, 965, has been forever retired. The toll-free number dedicated to accident-related calls will be staffed by more than a thousand specially trained reservations agents in Dallas.

The process of compiling the passenger list is already underway, involving comparing ticket coupons and other data from the departure gate to the list of the passengers holding reservations or waiting for standby seats for the flight. Sometimes, a standby passenger is issued a boarding pass but then decides to go to another gate and get on the waiting list for an earlier flight. This process of flight roulette is used by some *non-revs*, the airline employees flying on personal business. Although it's a practice not permitted by the airlines, and one they could lose their job over, there are some employees who check multiple gates and loads, then list themselves more than once in an effort to increase their odds of getting a seat.

Once this preliminary list is compiled, it is released internally so the families can be notified. The Emergency Response Team will notify the next of kin using the emergency phone numbers the passenger has given the airline prior to flight and from any numbers provided by inbound-calling family members who have seen the crash coverage on television. If foreign nationals were aboard the flight, the airline transmits a list of their names to the State Department. In addition, the entire passenger list is forwarded to the director of family-support services at the National Transportation Safety Board and any other federal agencies necessary. All of this information will tie back to the airline's Emergency Response Team, and a team member or two is assigned to each family right away to assist with personal issues and logistical support.

The pilot makes the landing announcement, and before I know it we're at the gate and into the bustling terminal at Miami International. A woman pushes by me lugging a shopping bag stuffed with colorful packages, reminding me again what day it is. A swarm of voices talk about the crash, and airport employees discuss the mountain and the search for the black box. It's almost three in the afternoon when I find my way to the small room near the departure gates in the main terminal in Miami, where other employees have gathered. I slide my identification badge through the security device and the door clicks open, granting me access to a room filled with people: employees taking breaks or waiting for flights. Someone has taped a passenger list for 965 on the wall behind the door, along with the State Department report that was issued earlier in the day, attesting that at least forty-eight of the passengers on board were U.S. citizens. Most of the others were Latin Americans headed home for the Christmas holiday, a fact that has been confirmed by reports of a scattering of Christmas packages across the ground near the crash site.

At the rear of the room, every cubicle and computer is occupied as the employees check flights, work on files, and speculate about the cause of the crash. The plane went down in an area dominated by leftist guerrillas, but officials continue to maintain that there is no evidence of an explosion on the plane and that all radio systems were operating normally. Rescue teams searching for the wreckage found only the tail section on the side of a mountain. It was nine in the morning, and they found the fuselage later, after an exhaustive search. The plane came to rest thirteen miles east of the normal flight path, and it is presumed that most of the passengers are dead.

The primary command centers established for this incident are in Colombia and Dallas, but there will also be satellite command centers created during the activation, including one at the makeshift morgue. The morgue is where rescue and medical workers will assemble to work on victim recovery and identification, and will be the initial activity point. A morgue is normally a precise operation involving professionally trained team members who will maintain constant communication and briefings on passenger remains with executives stationed at other command centers. Since the first and foremost concern of all families will be whether their loved one has survived, the transition a victim makes from *passenger* to *deceased* will be delicate and sensitive. It has to be expeditious and it has to be done in a caring fashion. Studies have shown that the way an airline handles this process with the family members makes a critical difference in the litigation pursued and the overall general public view of how the carrier handled the disaster.

*   *   *

In Miami, not much is happening on Christmas night. Normally there would be employee parties, trees decorating every airline's offices, and employees decked out in Santa pins and sweaters. But this Christmas is different. The mood is pensive. Throughout the system, flags are flown at half-mast, and the focus is on the families of those who have died. Airline employees are glued to television monitors in airport offices, hoping for an update on the cause of the crash.

I ask a gate agent for directions to the Admirals Club, the private frequent-flyer facility where I have been told to wait until my flight to Cali departs. Emergency Response Team members have been positioned there throughout the night, waiting for parents, spouses, and other loved ones trying to make their way to Cali. We will meet them at their arrival gates with electric carts and personally escort them to the club to avoid the confusion of the crowds and any possibility of an encounter with the press.

Before I leave the employee holding room, I sign in to a vacant computer, entering the code to get into my personal activation record. The records are confidential, and it is here where I will update any information pertaining to my travel to and from the crash location and other important details about the tasks I have performed. The computer records are accessed with a series of confidential characters followed by my employee number. The passwords change with every activation and this one is so unique it makes me laugh. Updates on the crash activities can be sent and received on a daily basis, so the computer records come in handy, because employees all over the world can communicate privately and for free from any major airport.

Sabre is one of the most sophisticated computer databases in the world. It is well known that the security is so stringent in Tulsa that a series of tests are required to enter, including a body weight test to make sure an individual is the same weight exiting as they were when they entered and an eye retina test that determines identification using an retina-scanning device. The database is private and available only to the employees who work for the airline, all of whom have passed a series of rigorous background, criminal, and psychological tests before being hired.

I log out of the computer and open the event log contained in my Emergency Response Team manual. Every team member must carry this log with them to create a continual summary of their activities. The event log is really a series of forms containing dates, events, communication with families, and any other details that the airline can keep on record long after the activation is complete. These records are filed under every incident flight number for future reference. At this point I have nothing significant to report, so I log a brief summary of the past twenty-four hours and make a note of the cab expense. After I return home, I'll submit a formal expense report with all receipts attached for reimbursement. I flip the manual to the first section and read through the activation checklist. If there is anything I still need, now is my last chance to find it. The checklist contains the basics for travel, such as a passport, company identification badge, special Emergency Response Team identification, several changes of clothes, toiletries, medical prescriptions, appropriate funeral attire, credit cards, stationery with airline letterhead, and small things like pens, pencils, and paper clips.

The to-do list includes items such as paying a month's bills in advance, just in case we are gone for any length of time, suspending the mail and newspaper services, and arranging for a pet sitter.

I make a few last-minute phone calls to tie up loose ends: one to pay an overdue credit-card bill, another to fill a prescription that a friend could ship to me if needed, and a third to leave a message for my mother, who will remain anxious until I arrive safely home.

I push open the door to the terminal, where the crowds are increasing.

"Excuse me!" The woman tries to pass, catching her foot against the door before it can close. She is short and middle-aged, with pale brown hair curled under all around her head.

"I'm sorry," I say, guarding the doorway. "Can I see your identification card?" She could be an airline employee, but she could just as easily be a member of the press.

She fumbles through the purse strapped to her shoulder, and several shards of paper fall to the floor. Her hands tremble.

"It's in here somewhere," she says, shaking her head. "I've been traveling all day, I just got back from the crash site."

"Are you with the ERT?"

"Yes, I just came back. I was down there working the crash but they sent me home." She thrust her hand deeper into the vinyl purse in frustration. A hotel matchbook and several pesos fall out.

"Oh boy, I know it's here. I just got off the flight. Didn't want to wear it on the plane in case there were reporters."

"Why did they send you home?"

"I don't know, I did everything…" her eyes well up.

A pilot in full uniform moves past us, swipes his card, and enters.

"Why don't we move over here," I suggest, pointing to a row of connected plastic chairs. We step away from the door and lower ourselves into the seats.

"Here it is!" She holds the badge in the air. The woman in the picture is blonde, but has the same hairstyle and outdated eyeglasses overwhelming her face. It is definitely the same woman.

"Sharon, nice to meet you." I say, extending my hand.

"Nice to meet you, too. Are you on the team?"

"Yes. I'm headed down there on tonight's flight."

She scans the terminal and turns all the way around to see who is seated in the row of chairs behind us. No one is there.

"You got a minute?" Her voice lowers to an intriguing whisper.

"Sure, actually I've got quite a while before my flight leaves."

"Maybe I can help you out. This your first time?"

"Yes."

Her eyes widen. She leans in and clutches the purse in her lap. "When I got there, I checked into the hotel and went straight to the command center, at the Intercontinental Hotel in Cali. You should see all the hotel staff catering to our employees. They've really bent over backwards. The one running the show at the command center there is an older gentleman who runs a pretty tight ship. He's been with the company for years, kind of a right-hand man to the Chairman. He's very organized. Anyways, a group of our people were headed to the mountain and before I knew it I was in a van going to the morgue."

"We already found a morgue location?" She is wearing jeans, white sneakers without a mark on them, and a floral cotton shirt. She has on an outfit I can't imagine in a morgue.

"Yes," she whispers. "An old soccer stadium up there. Everything happened so fast and I was one of the first there. But anyways, they found the body of the pilot and copilot and told me to guard them through the night. They didn't have anything over them, they were just stacked on the floor and I had to make sure no one came in and disturbed them."

I do not say anything. Her story is hard to believe.

"I don't think it's the local custom to cover the bodies of the deceased," she continues, "but besides that there weren't any body bags because, of course, no one expected the crash out there in the middle of the jungle. When I left they were calling the Red Cross to help get some shipped in."

I try to imagine her there, but it seems inconceivable. Surely she had never witnessed anything like it before.

"There were local kids and other people stealing things from the ground, and someone came in and tried to get to the pilots, and I just came unglued. He tried to take a watch from the pilot and I started screaming until he ran away." Her eyes fill up again. "So then I find out they have arranged to have me sent home. I can't believe it…I want to be there helping and they think I'm having some sort of breakdown or something."

"It must have been hard to deal with what you've seen."

She looks away. "It'll be harder to deal with it sitting at home in my apartment," she says quietly. "I have no idea what I'm going to do tonight."

She stands, fastening the long purse strap diagonally across the front of her chest.

"I'd better get going. My bags are probably in baggage claim by now."

"Take care of yourself." I do not know what else to say.

As I watch her walk away, her shoulders turned down and head lowered, I am overcome by a sudden sadness. I imagine her in a tiny apartment with a frozen dinner. The silence is deafening, the images of the crash invade. The pilots, the looters, the crash. The sights, the sounds, the confusion. I do not know if this is what she faces, but this is how I imagine it.

I walk through the terminal to the Admirals Club, which takes me fifteen minutes to find. I ride the elevator up a level to the main entrance and show my badge to the girl manning the desk inside. There is no one else standing in line, so she offers to brief me on the club's occupants. We walk out into the main sitting area, which is

furnished elegantly around the needs of the upscale business traveler. A big-screen television commands the center of the room and
several chunky chairs have been positioned around it. On a far wall,
a long granite bar is stocked with coffee, tea, and cookies.

"That family is traveling on to Cali," she says quietly, pointing out a
well-dressed couple in their fifties. The man is tall with a wiry build and
sits with his arms and legs crossed. He stares out the window onto a tarmac covered with jets, and his wife sits beside him, saying nothing.

"Their son was on the flight," says the girl. "I've turned off the televisions in every area so that they don't have to be subjected to the
news." She checks a printout of the passenger list from Flight 965
and gives me their last name. "Maybe you could check on them in a
half hour or so, see if they need anything."

"What if someone wants the television turned back on?" I ask.

"I guess it's alright. We have to do whatever they want, make them
feel as comfortable as possible. If they want it on, turn it on."

As she says this, a lanky young man in a baseball cap and college
sweatshirt rises from a patterned chair, walks to the television, and
turns it on.

"That's a family from California," the girl says. "His sister and her
kids were on the flight."

We continue to walk, and in each room there are more. Asleep in
chairs, sprawled on the floor, sitting at the bar drinking beer. The
club is eerily silent and the air is thick. The usual activity and noises
associated with ringing cell phones and businessmen tapping on
laptops has been replaced by a darkness difficult to define. We weave
through each room in the club until we have come full circle and
are standing at the check-in desk again.

"Basically, you can just make sure they're comfortable," the girl
says. "Every once in awhile, just ask them if they need anything.
Bring them a Coke, food, whatever they need."

I make another pass around the club, walking slowly through the
chairs, turning over newspapers with headlines about the crash. I

pick up some empty plates and crumpled napkins from a counter covered with complimentary cheeses and sandwiches and pour myself a cup of coffee from the pot.

I ask two families if I can get them something to drink or eat, but no one wants anything. The young man in the ballcap stares at me and does not answer. An older woman sitting alone waves me away with the back of her hand. Instantly I feel like an intruder. She is dressed in mismatched but expensive clothes, as if she had gotten dressed in the dark, after a call in the middle of the night. A Louis Vuitton bag rests at her feet. Her hair is straight and unfinished and she wears no makeup, though she looks like the kind of woman who is normally never without it.

I move to the back room, behind a door reserved for waitresses and Admirals Club employees, thinking about the unexpected tragedy that awaits me in my future. How will I look when the call comes in the middle of the night? I doubt that I'll care.

In the back room there is a small kitchen and a table covered with turkey, mashed potatoes, and picked-over cookies. Someone has posted a notice on a cork bulletin board by the sink:

*We are so sorry for your loss. Please know you are in our thoughts. With love, the employees of Delta airlines.*

Beside the notice is a newspaper article about the crash, and I pull out the tack and read through it. I place the article back on the board when I am done and pull myself onto the kitchen counter and just sit. Inside, I am numb, overcome with a loneliness so heavy I could suffocate.

The door creaks open and a heavyset woman in a Christmas sweater steps inside.

"Help yourself to the Christmas dinner," she says cheerfully. "It's about as good as we're going to get." She hands me a paper plate and in a flash she is gone, taking the air in the room with her.

I pick at the turkey and make a plate of cold mashed potatoes and stuffing, but my heart aches. Maybe it is because for a brief moment I had forgotten it was Christmas, or the realization that all across America there were families sitting down at the table together for dinner.

Outside the door, just four feet from where I sit, are people whose entire lives have been altered, and I wonder if Christmas can ever be the same for them again. I put down the plate and sit there on the counter, my hands gripping the edge.

When it is time to board my flight, I grab the duffle bag and make my way through the terminal, thinking about Sharon, the woman who had guarded the pilots' bodies. I berate myself for letting her go without getting her help. *I should have told someone.* I should have walked her to a counselor; I should have prevented her from going home unattended. What if she cannot handle it, what if she finds life too hard to bear? Other disaster-recovery workers have ended up in mental hospitals, and some have taken their lives.

I push the thought away and tell myself that not everyone solves problems that way. She will go back to her apartment, shower, cry a little, but move on with her normal life. She will get help if she needs it, and she will carry on. I board the plane and by the time I have settled into my seat I've convinced myself that everything will be okay. Let Sharon be a lesson, I tell myself. When I get there, I'll keep my emotions in check, no matter how bad it gets. I will not be sent home.

*　*　*

The takeoff is smooth and soon we are floating effortlessly in the sky. I recline my seat and glance at the young man beside me, a large black man who grips the armrest with both hands. He is bulky and muscular and wears baggy jeans and a black ski hat pulled down over his ears. A thick gold chain with some sort of astrological emblem dangles from his neck. Beside him, his son, a tiny replica dressed just like him, watches the clouds outside the window.

"They always do that?" the man asks, pointing to the flight attendant. She holds the plastic instruction card above her head and gestures to the diagram of the airplane in the center of it. She flashes a smile, folds open the card, and points inside to another diagram of the interior of an aircraft.

"Do what?" I ask.

"They always hold it up like a prize or something? Like *Wheel of Fortune?*"

"Always," I reply, laughing. "It's mandatory on all flights."

He scans the cabin nervously.

"Is this your first time flying?"

"Yeah," he says. "You flown before?"

"Yes."

I think of a million things to tell him starting with everything will be okay, that it's more dangerous to ride in a car than in a plane, and all the reassuring things that I have ever heard before. But at this point in time I do not believe any of it, so I say nothing at all.

"Why are you going to South America?" he asks, breaking the silence.

"I'm going to help out some friends down there." It's the truth, and even if it weren't it would have to be. I cannot tell him more than that.

"And you?"

"My boy's mother is there. She's a Latin girl. We met in the States but now she lives with her parents down there. He's gonna go live with her for awhile."

"I see."

"Hey, did you hear about that crash down there? Man, I hope that's not us."

"Crashes are pretty rare...I think we're safe," I say, smiling reassuringly.

We talk for a short time until the beer he has ordered takes effect and he is fast asleep. I stretch out and close my eyes in an attempt to focus on the task ahead, though there is no way I can predict what will happen. I once read a story about a prisoner of war who had developed a mental exercise to cope with the stress of the unknown during captivity. He had been held against his will for years in a small, dingy cell infested with rats, and each day had no idea whether he would live or die. The unknown was killing him, even worse than the actual conditions, so he decided to do something about the terrible stress affecting his survival. In the years after he escaped he shared his secret. He had survived the boredom and horrid conditions by using his mind and creating happy images that he could replay over and over again at will. He trained himself to pull up one of these images whenever a negative thought or experience occurred. In essence, he did everything possible to keep the negative images out by bringing positive ones in, and in doing so he held on to hope. This simple exercise helped him overcome the endless days of depression he was destined to suffer.

I pull out my leather-bound journal and decide to try this exercise to prepare myself for the difficult days ahead. I begin to think of happy events that I'll recall like video clips when I need them. I write them down in my notebook:

1. *The day I discovered that I was not an only child*

2. *Spending time with my new brothers at my grandfathers farm*

Both are recent memories, and when I recall the day that I found my brothers, just a few months ago, the sadness of the woman in the airport disintegrates. I envision the three of us laughing together, and I can remember exactly how I felt when I saw that they looked like me, talked like me, thought like me. I can hear the happiness in their voices and feel the comfort of knowing I'll never be alone again. I settle back into the seat and think about the past. My father had disappeared when I was seven. My mother had no other children. Throughout my childhood I asked her about my father many times, but hit a brick wall. No one in my family would explain the circumstances of his absence and he was pushed away, as if he had never existed. Years later I dug deeper, researching until I located my father's name and finally, to my dismay, his obituary. He was dead, but, to my surprise, two boys were listed as his surviving sons.

Through my brothers, I've been given the answers I had always longed for: the knowledge of my father's tumultuous life, his suicide, and the fact that he did not abandon just me. There were three of us now.

I know that I have been given a gift—the second half of my life with the family I have always wanted. But now I am headed to a place where I will work with those who will spend the second part of their lives without the family they have always known. Which is the better option? I spend nearly an hour pondering this one profound thought and accept a glass of wine from the flight attendant. It helps me relax and I slip into a half-sleep, closing my eyes and imagining happy scenario number two, my grandfather at the farm sitting on his favorite spot on the porch, smoking a cigar. My brother and I have brought him cigars from New York City, but he refuses them when he discovers they're fifty dollars apiece. He will only smoke two-dollar cigars, and anything else is ridiculous, he says.

I spin around the yard on the four-wheel, all-terrain vehicles my grandfather keeps in his barn, racing my brothers, who are as competitive as I am. I have never done this before, and it is a moment I will never forget. The one who loses will be mad at the other two, but it won't last long. My grandfather shakes his head at our recklessness as we race around the barn, getting airborne on the hill in the front yard. I'm going the fastest, but the turn is too sharp and my ATV dives into the ditch by the gravel road. My brothers laugh and taunt me unmercifully as my grandfather fires up the tractor to tow me out.

When I open my eyes, the airplane cabin is engulfed in darkness. A man travels slowly down the aisle and smiles at me, then turns around and walks by once again. He has striking brown eyes and a firm jaw, and I guess him to be about thirty-four. When he stares too long, I look away, but he passes again slowly, and then stops next to my seat.

"May I sit here for a moment?" he asks, pointing to the empty seat in the aisle across from me.

When I see him closer, I immediately recognize him as John Quinones, a correspondent for *20/20*, a major network news show. I have seen him many times on television, giving reports about various tragedies in the world. He sits and hands me his card.

"I can't talk to reporters. I'm sorry."

He is interesting and successful and someone I'd like to converse with, but I cannot take the risk. If I'm spotted engaging in a lengthy conversation with the media, my trip will be very brief.

"What hotel are you staying at?" he asks politely. He is interested only in the story.

"How do you know I'm with the airline?" I am dressed in civilian clothing, no identification, and my manual is camouflaged.

"I have my ways," he smiles.

"I'm sorry...but I can't talk to you. You know I can't..."

He brushes a hand through his hair. "I understand. But if you change your mind, give me a call. My hotel number is on the back of the card."

The minute he returns to his seat, a flight attendant approaches. Every crewmember has been advised of the Emergency Response Team members on board.

"You're going to the crash site? Do you know who you were just talking to? Mind if I sit?" I do not know which question to answer first. She smiles at the empty seat and sits without waiting for my reply.

"Are you a flight attendant?" she asks. It is a common question, one that I am used to. I have found during my career that even the employees of the airline assume that you're a flight attendant if you're a woman under thirty and remotely attractive. People outside the airline industry assume there are only two jobs in the airline— flight attendant and pilot—which is why I have learned not to say that I work for an airline unless I'm prepared to give a ten-minute explanation on my job as a sales manager. In actuality, the airline is a society in itself, with several jobs and communities. The airline employs more than a hundred thousand people across the world, in a variety of vocations. There are attorneys, assistants, a full real-estate department that negotiates leases on hangars, offices, and mainte-nance facilities, and a variety of other careers available. In any large airline, there are staff psychologists, physicians, writers, and janitors, many of them women.

I tell the flight attendant that I'm a sales manager, and that I work marketing the airline to corporations, an answer that seems sufficient enough.

"Can I talk to you about the crash?" she probes.

"Actually, I've got some required reading to do before I get there. I've really got to spend time studying."

Emergency Response Team members are forbidden to talk about any aspect of the crash during an actual activation, unless it's with someone involved in the accident investigation. This includes flight attendants, I want to tell her.

"You know he's got a whole camera crew back there," she contin-ues. "If they even open a camera bag, I'll have the pilot confiscate all their equipment. We have the authority to do that, you know."

"Yes, I know."

"So are you nervous? What's your assignment?"

A man with a large black news camera slides into an empty aisle behind her and positions the lens out the aircraft window. He then turns the camera to the inside of the cabin, scanning the passengers. The attendant is oblivious.

"I've got a girlfriend," she says breathlessly, "a flight attendant out of Miami who was almost scheduled on that flight."

"I'm sorry but I've really got to get this reading done. And you probably need to take care of that." I point to the camera and her eyes widen in horror.

"Sir, you can't do that!" she shouts. "Sir, put that camera away!"

She covers the lens with her hand, but it is too late. The camera-man has gotten the footage he needed, of the inside of the cabin. It is footage that will be replayed over and over again on the nightly news and a shot that has not been sanctioned by corporate communications. In seconds, the camera is back in the bag and the cameraman is in his seat. The flight attendant rushes to the front of the aircraft and disappears into the cockpit. Moments later she reappears with a pilot and takes him back to the row with the camera crew. The pilot exchanges a few stern words and warns them that their equipment will be confiscated if the camera comes out again.

The passengers in nearby rows stare at the commotion but everyone understands what it's about. We are on the same flight that went down in the middle of the night several days ago, and it's hard not to think about it. Soon, we will all be able to see the crash site from the sky.

# chapter eight

# Buga

The night is at its blackest when the jet sets down at the airport in Cali and silences its massive engines. Outside the airplane window, the tarmac is alive. When the entry door disengages, I follow the long line of bleary-eyed passengers to the front of the plane and step outside onto the aluminum platform at the top of the stairwell. The warm air rushes in and the heat ripples the blacktop below, which is dotted with locals dressed in the ill-fitting polyester pants and button-downs the airline has provided them. The pants are blue, like in the States, and the shirts white. A simple uniform.

The night air is thick. I take a deep breath, filling my lungs with the sweet scent of papaya. The crash site was not visible from the airplane window because the pilots had been informed of the exact location of the wreckage and had been told to take the necessary precautions to avoid it by traveling a different flight path.

The Cali airport terminal is small and packed with people, some holding signs. The crowd of passengers pushes towards baggage claim, where two airline employees answer questions and give directions. In the corner against one wall, a woman in a professional black suit flips through pages attached to a clipboard. She wears a gold name badge on her lapel and the small green

Emergency Response Team sticker we are required to wear at all times.

"Excuse me," I interrupt, "are you with the Emergency Response Team?"

"Your name?" she asks.

Her eyes are hazel, pretty if they hadn't been traced in severe black eyeliner on both the upper and lower lids. It is a style from before my time, when the women wore sultry raccoon eyes with Jackie-O suits. Her face is taut, as if a surgeon has attempted to help her fight time, which had already turned against her.

I give her my name and smile respectfully, seeing into a moment twenty years forward when I will stand in her shoes, subjected to women decades younger but equal in professional stature. Their skin will be clearer and tighter, their attitudes carefree, unmarred by the inevitable losses that advancing years bring.

She checks my name against a list. "We're going to the hotel in vans but we have to wait for the other arrivals. You can wait over there." She points to a small group gathered against the wall. Most look like they have slept in their clothes for six hours.

"Excuse me," I feel a light tap on my shoulder and turn to face a girl in her late thirties with a black nylon backpack slung over her shoulder.

"Yes?"

"I overheard you say you're with the Emergency Response Team," she says. "I'm not crazy about sitting around here, so I'm going to grab a taxi and head over to the command center. You're welcome to share a cab if you want."

Her dark hair is pulled into a tight ponytail and her pants are made of parachute material, the kind hikers wear. She looks as if she knows her way around a mountain.

"Sure, if you know where we're going," I reply.

"I've got the address. I figure it's better than waiting an hour. I'm Barbara, by the way. Hartford sales."

"Tammy Kling, Dallas sales."

A crowd has gathered at the exit, greeting incoming passengers with shouts and signs. We step past them to the curb where several taxi drivers compete for our attention.

"Missus, you need a ride?" one shouts.

"*Hola, senorita!*" says another.

"Taxi!"

Signs bob in the air. The one who shouts the loudest is small in stature, with strong features and skin the color of chocolate. He wears plastic flip-flops and a Mickey Mouse T-shirt, and pushes forward, ignoring the others.

"Miss, I have good car," he says, stepping forward. "I take you where you need to go." The man reaches for my bag and smiles, exposing large teeth.

"We go," he says, nodding towards the vehicle. I glance back at Barbara, motioning her over. The car has a significant indent on one side, and the door groans in protest when he pulls it open. I slide into the back and Barbara pushes in behind me.

"Hotel Intercontinental, *por favor*," she says.

"*Si, senorita.* Have you been there before?"

"*Si*," she says, though she hasn't. She gives me a look that tells me she has lied to make certain we are not taken advantage of. I am grateful for her street smarts, which will ensure we aren't driven all over the city of Cali en route to the hotel.

The road leading out of the airport is crowded with scooters, and locals are piled onto the back in twos and threes carrying plastic bags containing their possessions. On one scooter, an old woman sits sideways in a colorful skirt, while the driver navigates the chaotic traffic. As we approach town, the street corners are dark and I cannot help but think of the people who would have taken this journey into the city at the exact same time had their plane landed that night like it should have. The passengers would have been greeted at the airport by friends and family, or picked up by a taxi and taken to a hotel. Either way, they would have seen the same crowded terminal, the large tree at the corner of the airport exit, and the dark winding roads into the city.

We drive through dim alleys and arrive at an intersection where soldiers stand on each corner with machine guns strapped across their chests. They wear fatigues and heavy black boots, and some hold their guns upright, as if poised to fire at any moment. I reach for the lock on my door and press it down quietly. The car rolls to a stop at the traffic light. The soldier standing on the curb turns and, to my horror, bends at the waist to peer into our car. Our eyes meet, and in his eyes I see nothing but small brown pools. His gaze is direct and penetrating, absent of emotion. I look away towards Barbara, but she is focused on something in the distance, outside her window. The light remains red for an eternity, and though I do not look out the window again, I can feel the soldier's stare. I nudge Barbara with my elbow. Gratefully, the light turns and the taxi accelerates.

"It's that platinum blond hair," she says. "It draws a lot of attention, especially down here. You might consider wearing a ballcap."

I laugh.

"I'm serious. We'll be all over this city and you'll stand out like a sore thumb. A lot of blondes wear hats in strange parts of the world. You don't want to draw attention to yourself."

I fold my hands into my lap, suddenly self-conscious of the wedding ring I should have left at home. I know better than to wear jewelry on a trip like this, but it was one detail I had missed.

"Have you worked an activation before?" she asks.

"No, this is my first."

"So you're a neophyte. Well, you're in for an awakening. This activation is pretty serious. We'll be dealing with a lot of sad and hysterical people."

"Sounds like you've been through it."

"Yes," she says slowly. "But it was a long time ago. I had even considered withdrawing from the program afterward, but never got around to it. After so many years went by without an accident, I just felt like I'd never be called up again." She takes a long breath. "I guess I was wrong."

The driver halts to a stop in front of a tall building with flags waving at the entrance, and I exhale with a sigh of relief. The hotel is not what I had expected. It is a surprisingly modern structure, with lofty doors leading to a lobby that seems to mirror all of the conveniences of a hotel in the United States. Through the glass windows I can see a bellman, a check-in desk, and a large table covered with a floral arrangement.

I grab my duffle bag and hang back while Barbara gives the driver several American dollars. He smiles gleefully and hauls her suitcase from the trunk. Inside, an attractive hotel clerk stands behind the check-in counter as if she has been anticipating our arrival.

"Yes?" she says. Her hotel jacket is pressed and tailored, covering a matching gabardine skirt and flesh-colored hose. Her long black hair is pulled taut into a slick ball at the nape of her neck and secured with a tortoise-shell clasp.

"We're with the airline," I offer. "We need to go to the command center."

A brochure on the counter depicts the hotel's amenities, none of which I expect to see. There is a workout center, steam room, and resort-style pool.

The girl lifts her hand and, with one gesture, summons a compact woman leaning against a pillar in the lobby. She is unobtrusive, with jet-black hair and black eyes, and greets us both with a firm handshake. She motions us to the elevator and presses a button for the fifteenth floor.

On fifteen, she escorts us to the room housing the command center, a vast connection of hotel rooms that have been opened up and connected to create one giant space on the top floor of the hotel. Inside, twenty or thirty airline employees are engaged in various tasks, but the room is strangely quiet. We move in, and are approached by a man who asks both of us for our identification badges. He scans them and gives them back.

"I'm Jason," he says. "I'm working as the administrator here today. Why don't you ladies follow me and I'll get you all set up. I'm sure there's something we can find for you to do."

He leads us around the room until I have met so many people that it will be impossible to remember their names. The last introduction is to George Jones, director of the emergency operation here in Cali, and a man whose name I have heard frequently over the years. He's a towering man in his late fifties whose normal job entails overseeing the general operations of the company. It's a powerful position, and he can often be seen on CNN giving an update on the state of the airline.

"Tammy's a team leader," Jason explains. "She took over for Betty Lancefield after Betty took early retirement."

George glances at me briefly. "Good. I'm sure your team members will be arriving in the next few days and then they can be assigned various tasks. We've got plenty to do here. We'll give them your hotel room number so they can call you if they need anything."

I nod confidently, though I doubt I'm prepared to direct the members of my team. I realize that George probably has no idea that this is my first activation, not that the specifics matter at this point. Here we will all need to focus on the tasks we're given and be acutely aware of our actions. It is here that a career could be ruined or elevated, because there will be so much personal contact with the highest-level executives in the company.

Mr. Jones's eyes dart like mosquitoes, landing on everyone in the room. He talks into a hand-held radio and then moves away to a corner to finish the conversation.

"You're staying here at this hotel," Jason tells Barbara. "You can go ahead and go downstairs to check in."

He searches through a paper with a list of typewritten names.

"You're not on the list," he says, eyeing the name on my badge again. "You must be at another hotel."

"Are you serious?"

I envision myself in a seedy hotel in a scary part of town, as if the idea of being a young woman alone in a hotel in Colombia isn't scary enough. I recall the words my mother had said when I called her to tell her I was going to Cali—words I had dismissed. *They kidnap tourists there all the time, especially Americans.*

"Don't worry," Jason says. "The remaining rooms here have all been reserved for the families of the victims, so we've arranged to have the overflow of our employees housed at another property down the road. I just have to figure out which property has the rooms. Get back to me before the end of the night."

"Alright."

"I'll take good care of you," he adds with a wink. "Have you met your buddy yet?"

"No."

He waves a hand. "Don't worry. You will. It's more of a babysitter thing anyways." He rolls his eyes.

The buddy program was created to make certain all team members are protected emotionally. We are teamed up with another individual who can relate to what he or she is going through. In training, we were told that every Emergency Response Team member activated would be assigned a buddy, and every team member will *be* a buddy. The buddy's role is to help their buddy talk through the events of each day, and to make sure that the rules and regulations of the team are being followed. The buddy is the one person that each of us will spend the most time with.

"You'll need a Go-Kit," Jason says. "Go over to that table and get one."

He points to a table across the room, where a woman who has been assigned the task of doling out supplies puts together several small boxes containing everything we will need while we're here.

She gives me a form to fill out for a cell phone and asks me to complete it.

"The serial number is on the back of the telephone," she says. "Write it on the form in the column under Serial Number, then sign your name beside it."

I do as I'm told and clip the phone and a pager she gives me to my waist. Jason is standing by a long conference table surrounded by people, and when he sees me he waves me over. In the center of the table are several plastic file boxes, and stacks of documents.

"These guys are with the insurance company," he says. "They're creating files on the Jim Johnsons, getting them ready for transport. You can help them out."

Although nothing had been mentioned about Jim Johnsons during training, I had heard the term at the command center in Dallas, and know enough to understand that it's a code we will use for precious cargo: the bodies of the deceased from the airplane crash. The *Jim Johnson* moniker was devised to differentiate a crash victim from a standard cargo shipment, such as a body unrelated to the crash being transported across the United States. The name Jim Johnson is etched on the outside of the wooden cargo box for shipment so that the airline employees on the tarmac at the arriving destination can be sensitive to its contents. While baggage handlers unload the cargo from the belly of the aircraft, it is likely that family members will be there to greet it, watching from a window in the airport. I gather from the number of people at the table that the insurance process is a complicated one.

"Have a seat," a man there says. He points to a stack of official-looking documents. "Sort through these and make sure every passenger file has one of these white papers in it. The main thing here is to make sure all of the paperwork is in order for the remains of each passenger to be shipped home."

I place the document, which looks like some sort of release form, in the first file. I pass the folder to the girl beside me, who takes a different document from a stack in front of her and does the same. When the file has reached the end of the table, a young man wearing a golf shirt places it into an alphabetized file box.

"Those secretarial skills are coming in handy, aren't they?" says the girl beside me. Her black hair is loosely pinned and several strands have fallen in her eyes. She wears khakis and brown loafers with a white button-down. Her name tag says Judy.

"Where you from?" she asks.

"Dallas."

"I hate Texas. My ex-husband is there."

I smile and continue the mundane task of stuffing folders.

"Bet you never thought you'd be spending your days filing," she says. "Exciting, isn't it?" She sniffs and wipes her nose with the back of her sleeve. "The identification process will take an eternity," she whispers. "Have you seen the crash site?"

"No, I just got here."

She shakes her head. "Nothing but fragments. Believe it or not, this is probably the most important job down here."

She points to a number on the outside of a file folder. "Every passenger has a case number, and every case number is recorded on the outside of a file. Inside the folder are the documents recording specific details about the passenger, and also official documents that will get them transported back to the United States. There's a lot that goes into it."

She explains that every Jim Johnson shipped will be accompanied by a file containing pertinent details, the passenger record from the airline, and insurance information. It's a long process that will continue for days and weeks, because a passenger cannot become a Jim Johnson until they have been officially identified. When the Jim Johnson is ready to be shipped, we'll assign an Emergency Response Team representative to greet the family on the other end. Sometimes the team member is invited to the funeral, but more often their role is to ensure that everything goes smoothly, assisting only when they're asked. It is a delicate balancing act, knowing when to help, and when to step out of the picture.

"Who are all these people?" I ask. It's obvious that the six men seated at the table are not airline employees. They are all dressed alike, in blue, button-down shirts.

"They're with the insurance company. The one at the end is internal, with our insurance and risk-management group. And the one over there is John North, director of our cargo division." She points to a man across the table. His head is down, and he's involved in a serious telephone conversation. The table in front of him is littered with coffee cups, one of them crammed with cigarette butts. He wears a denim shirt rolled at the sleeves, revealing tanned forearms. His hands are thick and weather-beaten, unlike the other men, who have manicured nails and long, slender fingers.

"He's the most important man at this table," she says. "He's in charge of getting all the bodies back to their owners."

"I can imagine the stress he's going through," I say.

"Yes, he's got a lot of pressure on him. Every parent wants their kid's body found and shipped home. He never says much."

John North takes a cigarette from the pack of Marlboros in his shirt pocket and sticks it in his mouth. He lights it without interrupting his call and inhales quickly. In the center of the room, a television blasts live coverage of the crash. There have been a handful of survivors, the reporter says for the umpteenth time. Footage of the downed aircraft has reached the United States, and pieces of the fuselage can be seen on every network, from a helicopter's aerial view. The network shows a clear image of the broken airplane lying in pieces on the side of the mountain, and remarkably, the airline logo is intact. I cringe because it seems as if it's the worst possible scenario for an airline—crash coverage with the broken fuselage lying on the ground in pieces and a shot of the airline logo playing over and over in all parts of the world. The airline logo shot stays for several seconds and the picture is clear. Even without audio, the viewer can see clearly who owns the shattered aircraft. It has been five days since the airplane has gone down, and on the ground near the wreckage tiny dots of people can still be seen from the sky.

Buga, the area of the jungle where the airplane has come to rest, is a small but mysterious town that was founded in the 1500s. Ancient legend has it that in 1570 the Señor de Los Milagros—Jesus Christ—made an appearance before a woman on the bank of the Rio Guadalajara. She and others began to experience miracles and cures for their illnesses and the town became a religious sanctuary. A magnificent church was created in his honor in the form of the Basilica del Señor de los Milagros, and in the square in front of it there are street vendors who sell wax body parts for those wishing to place an offering on the altar. The theory is to show Christ which part of the body is ailing so that He may perform a miracle, in a town that has become known for them.

Up on the mountain called El Deluvio, there have been four miracles, and they have instilled a sense of hope in all of us that perhaps there will be more. The survivor operation continues, although the remaining days will consist mainly of recovery. If a survivor is found, the rescue worker who has made the discovery will send an alert any way possible, but more than likely via hand-held radio. The survivor will be taken to University Hospital, where doctors will work to stabilize them. But for now there have been no other reportings of life. I overhear a staff member say that there have been more than forty major crashes in South America involving commercial airlines. Most of them were the result of pilot error. Many had miscalculated the mountainous peaks jutting up against the sky, discovering too late that they surround the aircraft at every turn.

Rescue workers have cordoned off the crash site and the process of recovering remains is in full swing. FBI officials have arrived at the airport and Emergency Response Team personnel will continue to shuttle them to the crash site. The FBI agents are special agents trained in crisis management and are primarily young and fit, having passed the minimum physical test of one hundred sit-ups, twenty pull-ups, and fifty push-ups necessary to be accepted. Unlike the Emergency Response Team personnel, they have been prepared for the physical exertion, and they have been trained in international terrorism, criminal investigation, and victim identification. The media has reported that unsigned letters had been faxed to newspapers warning of bombs against flights from Venezuela and Colombia, and though it is doubtful that the threats are linked to the crash, everything will be investigated.

*  *  *

John North stands in front of the television and crosses his arms. His eyes fixate on the young reporter who speculates about what happened. *Several survivors have been found,* she says, though so far, there have been only four.

"Jeezus!" he says, running a hand over the stubble on his jaw. "How many times are they going to show the plane?"

He pulls aside one of the men from the insurance company and asks him about a specific passenger file. He moves to our side of the table and sits down in an empty chair beside me, reading through a document. He raises his head.

"The average weight of a Jim Johnson is somewhere around 280 pounds," he says, "give or take fifty pounds." His eyes scan the faces at the table. "The transport box weighs about a hundred and then you've got the remains."

The table is quiet.

"But here," he continues, "the total weight is just over a hundred."

"Why?" I ask, and just as quickly it hits me.

"Because that's all there is left." He stares at me, his eyes dark.

# chapter nine

# Changed Lives

At two in the morning, I make my way downstairs, through the hotel lobby and the maze of sad faces. I walk slowly, avoiding eye contact, feeling so exposed to the awareness that tragedy is just a second away. The families gather in corners, most of them sleeping in chairs, waiting. They are now more than just emergency contacts on a computer printout. Now they are faces, and lives forever changed. A woman sits on a chair in the corner. She's about seventy, with a pleasant face and floral print dress. I study her and think that she's too fragile to be here, and that no one should be subjected to such misery in the twilight of their lives. I picture her home, on the front porch of her house in the country, canning or knitting or tending the garden, but anywhere but here.

"Miss, can you help me?" I turn to face a man with graying hair. His hand grips my wrist, but his face is drawn and filled with a sense of urgency. I do not pull away.

"I'm Heath Elleson and my son Dan was on your flight." He says it quickly, as if he's said it a number of times already. "You're with the airline, aren't you? I was wondering if you have any more information for me."

He hands me a photograph of a young man wearing a graduation gown and black cap. The tassel is gold.

"This is my son," he says, pushing it towards me.

"He's very handsome," I reply, only because it's the first thing that comes to mind. "He looks like you."

The man smiles. "This is my son," he repeats.

"I'm so sorry." I take in a deep breath. There has been no more additional information on the passengers, and now, in the middle of the night, everyone is winding down. Rescue workers are still busy on the mountain, working around the clock, but for a family in search of a loved one, the wait is impossible to understand. I look into the man's frantic eyes and think, *What do you say when there is nothing to say at all?*

"Who's your Emergency Response Team liaison?" I ask.

His hand loosens from my arm and he lifts it slowly, pointing to a girl across the room, who I recognize from the command center.

"Over there." His fingers shake violently, and I pretend not to notice, just as I do with my grandfather who can't hold a coffee cup anymore without the coffee spilling out over the sides.

"Let me ask her," I say. "She should have more information."

"She doesn't know a damn thing," he says angrily. "Never mind." He thrusts the photo in his pocket and walks away, and when I look again his liaison has witnessed the exchange. In seconds, she is in front of me.

"He's in shock," she says. "I'll take care of it. He's been asking any-one and everyone with a badge for information. There's just nothing I can tell him right now."

*  *  *

Outside at the curb, the bellman hails a cab. My head throbs and the night air seems surreal, black and scented with orange. Cars pass on the road in front of the hotel, quick blurs of light unaware of the hour. The taxi is blue, not yellow, and the driver accelerates through side streets and empty alleys flanked by large concrete buildings. We stop in front of a small hotel, and I think I've slept half the way because I can't remember the ride.

The clerk at the front desk is polished, and welcomes me in English, inviting me to take a look around the lobby, which is filled with antiques. The hotel has a spa, she explains, and a small restaurant. A man in an oversized hotel jacket escorts me to my room on the second floor. Inside, I'm surprised to find a spacious yet intimate space exquisitely furnished.

A suitcase lies open on one of the beds, and an Emergency Response Team manual sits beside it, waiting to be read or stolen by housekeeping. I walk over to it and look at the page someone had been reading. It's the section on Latin America that I had started to review on the plane. I sit and read through it, learning about the subtle differences in communication in Colombia, which are very important when discussing sensitive topics. It is something we have already been trained to understand and something I had learned while studying books on international business in college. The male holds the dominant position in the head of the household, and as in some other countries, the older generations would tend to speak the native language only, while the younger generation would be fluent in English. Latin Americans generally speak faster and trust slower. During conversations with the victims' families, we were all advised to first direct conversations towards the male head of the household, who would direct most conversations on behalf of the entire family.

Across from the beds stands an ornate cherry armoire with elegant French detailing and a television tucked inside. I throw my duffle bag onto the available bed and prepare to unpack.

In the closet, there are several suits already hung in a neat row. They are dark, conservative, and a petite size four. The owner of the suits has hung them meticulously on padded satin hangers that all face in the same direction. In front of the suits hangs a single row of crisp, tailored shirts, two white and one blue. I hang my jacket on a hook and kick my shoes into the closet.

The bathroom is large and smells of a fresh shower. On the counter are two manila envelopes with black marker scrawled on the front. One is mine, the other is for someone named *Ms. Davis*.

Ms. Davis has already claimed her half of the bathroom, lining up several bottles of Clinique makeup on the countertop beside a hairbrush and comb. A makeup bag in the same pattern as the suitcase on the bed is filled with lotions and cleansers. I open it and look inside to see mascara, an eyelash curler, and some hair balm that the bottle describes as being for women of color. I unpack in no time, stuffing T-shirts and jeans into the armoire across from our beds. I have not packed any suits, and I have no idea if I'll need one. I undress and reach for the bathrobe in the closet, wrapping it around me. Soon I will meet my buddy, who I have determined is a professional, petite, African-American woman. But for now, I will have to wait.

# chapter ten

# Cali Command Center

On the morning of my second day in Cali, I am alone on my ride to the command center. My roommate was gone by the time I woke up, and the bathroom had been used but was put back together again in a fastidious fashion. The towels were folded, the counters clean, and any trace of water from the shower had been wiped away. The makeup bags were zipped and strategically placed, as if she had known I peeked into one.

I had slept soundly and did not hear her enter or leave, though I remember dreaming of people and voices, and rescuers finding many more survivors on the mountain, and then more survivors in the morgue who had previously been declared dead. In my dream, the survivors were awake and, much to the astonishment of the rescuers, just packed up their belongings that had been strewn across the ground and walked away as if nothing had happened. The dream unsettled me, and when I arrive at the command center the excitement I felt from the day prior has vanished.

The evening before, in an effort to understand the miracle that had occurred, I had checked the computer records of Flight 965 to determine where the survivors had been sitting. Although no one had shared it with us, I could see as I entered their names that Mercedes Ramirez, Mauricio Reyes, Gonzalo Dussan, and Michelle

Dussan, the survivors, had all been sitting in the same row.

Now they are all being treated at University Hospital in Cali, just minutes from the hotel. Mercedes Ramirez has undergone surgery for extensive abdominal injuries, and we have flown in her sister, Sylvia, the last remaining member of their nuclear family. We have assigned an Emergency Response Team member to work with them, as well as the other survivors and their families. When Sylvia had heard that someone named Mercedes had been pulled from the wreckage, she prayed for it to be her sister, because she knew that as close as her mother and father were, the death of the other would be too much to handle. She would wait until her sister's condition improved before telling her that their parents did not survive the crash.

Mr. Dussan, the thirty-six-year-old copy technician from New Jersey, has two broken vertebrae but is expected to make a full recovery. His daughter Michelle has lacerations to her face and body, but overall her condition is good. Reporters had interviewed Dussan and he was well aware that his son, Gonzalo Jr., had died on the operating table of cardiac arrest. The children's mother, Nancy Delgado, had not lived through the impact, but despite the losses, Mr. Dussan said that he would continue to go on, for the sake of his little daughter.

Mauricio Reyes has broken bones in his pelvis and face, and family members have maintained a happy vigil by his hospital bed, stunned at the miracle that he has made it out alive. The nineteen-year-old is talking and laughing and will leave the hospital and return to college and a bright future.

*  *  *

At the command center, George Jones is on the phone setting up the specifics of a conference call with someone in Dallas. Standing beside him is the same girl I had seen last night, an attractive brunette in her early twenties, with long, lustrous hair that seems to hypnotize the men in the room.

At 9:25, George pulls the group together and waits until everyone has quieted. The aircraft was a 757, he says, a plane that had accumulated thirteen thousand seven hundred eighty-two flight hours, and more than four thousand cycles, the term for takeoffs and landings. The airplane had Rolls Royce engines, and both had been in excellent condition. All maintenance checks were current. Just prior to departure the plane was loaded with forty-three thousand pounds of fuel. He describes the airport here, where the plane was supposed to land, as a building located in a long, narrow valley surrounded by mountains. Some of them reach altitudes of fourteen thousand feet. The airplane was only minutes away from landing when it crashed into one.

"Do you think it was caused by terrorist activity?" a woman asks.

"We don't know," George replies. "The plane was off course, that's all we can say for sure."

He reiterates that there have been only four survivors, and that the fifth, a boy who had lived through the impact, has been declared dead at the hospital.

"Listen up everybody," he demands. "Make sure you all take the notes, receipts, and documents about the crash and shred them every night and day. If there's anyone here who thinks they got anything sitting around in their hotel room, you're excused to go get it now. Reporters will be trying to pay housekeeping for the contents of your wastebaskets and anything else they can find about the crash."

Several people head for the door, hotel keys in hand.

I know that the investigation into this accident will continue for months and every detail will remain confidential until a task force has determined the final cause of the crash. The airline and aviation task force will work hard to ensure that leaks do not occur during the investigation. Meetings are confidential and all media questions are deferred until after the investigation has been formally completed. We have been advised that a rumor or false verdict on the cause of the crash could cause undue emotional harm to the family members of the passengers and create a barrage of incoming phone calls. Everyone will want more information on the new bit of information, true or false. One of the goals of our team is to protect the families from the rumors, the press, and any additional stresses they will face.

I file all day, helping to organize documents and running errands throughout the hotel until dinnertime, when an employee from room service arrives pushing a cart covered with fruit and cheese. It is followed by another with meats, rolls, and condiments for sand-wiches. Those of us working the command-center shift will eat hotel food for breakfast, lunch, and dinner. The workers on the ground will eat sandwiches made by volunteers and packed into lunch boxes for the trip to Buga. The rescue workers have been advised to wear hiking boots, long-sleeved shirts, and pants, although many have come just as they were when they first received word of the crash. Most are Colombian soldiers, and they trek to the wreckage up a mountain deep into the familiar jungle. The war here has been fought against the guerrillas and heavy drug trade, but today, the war is against time.

In the recovery process in the ensuing days, the location of the deceased passengers will be distinguished with a numbered marker placed in the ground. Photographs of the crash location will be taken and family members will be called. The initial goal of the rescue operation is to rescue as many people as possible, as effectively as possible, with the secondary goal being recovery. When the deceased are recovered, they will be transported to the makeshift morgue for further investigation.

It's rumored that a company we have contracted will be involved in the cleaning and restoration of the personal effects of passengers before they are returned to the families, and the personal effects, if any are found, will be verbally described to the next of kin, who will then determine if they want the object back. This will be done out of respect for the family, and if the items are indeed wanted, our air-line staff will return them and create an inventory of any other possessions. During the recovery process, every detail about the wreckage placement, cargo, and location of the bodies will help aid investigators in determining the cause of crash.

In the command center, Janice Sutton, a team member from New York, answers a call from a mother in the United States who is anxious to recover her daughter's remains. She places the woman on hold and repeats the request.

"The mother is frantic," Janice says. "Bordering on irate."

It has been several days since anyone has contacted the woman, and every time she calls the line is busy. The Emergency Response Team member handling her case has been helpful, but can tell her nothing of significance. She is at her wit's end and the only recourse the team member could find was to give the woman the direct number to the command center.

"Tell her we'll send them to her as soon as possible," John replies, "but I don't know if we've got them yet. Look for the file."

Janice searches through several file boxes but comes up empty. "I don't have anything. I think this is one we haven't recovered yet."

"Great," John says, "just great, and who the hell's giving out these internal numbers?"

The staff member shrugs. No one knows the answer to the question, and a family member calling directly to the command center is not within procedure. The family liaison should be following up with any questions the family has, but in some cases, the family and the liaison assigned to them do not get along. But I have seen already that in other cases, such as this one, it seems as if the liaison actually becomes an ally to the family, innocently and indiscreetly providing them with tidbits of inside information that will get them through the airline red tape.

John snatches the phone. "I'll talk to her," he says, taking the woman off hold. He explains that he will call her back later as soon as the correct paperwork is organized and a few other details have been cleared up. It is all he can do at this moment. I immediately understand why the methodical process exists. No family member should call the command center and risk being spoken to by someone like John, an abrupt operations person unfamiliar with his or her case. Whoever had given out the number had made a very big mistake.

At University Hospital, the information on the survivors is guarded and the nurses and doctors have been told not to release anything to anyone other than next of kin. Reporters have called posing as family members, trying anything to obtain information on the condition of the only passengers to survive the tragedy. Reporters have flown in from all over the world to get the story, and we have been told to be careful of reporters in disguise, and to prepare for any changes that might occur in the family members we are assigned to. In previous crashes, some families have rejected a team member, preferring to handle the post-crash details alone.

\* \* \*

Barbara, the woman I had met in the airport in Cali, works at the communication table handing out pagers and cell phones. When a team member turns one back in, she inventories it and records the serial number to prevent theft or loss. The command-center staff can contact us via the cell phones, which will work inside the country, and even for calls placed to the States. In training, we had been taught that communication would be the single most important factor in any airline rescue operation. It would be the process in which our team conveyed vital information to one another and on the families we were there to serve. How we talked to the family members of the crash victims would be essential, and a strong communication plan would make the difference between a positive or negative image of the airline. If the families feel that the airline has been responsive to them, and the media feels the airline has cooperated in providing updates after a crash, the general public will have an overall positive view of the way the airline has handled the tragedy.

Within the next few hours and days, some of us will receive families, which means we will need to contact a crash victim's loved ones to offer them one point of contact with the airline. If we are one of the team members assigned to this task, we will need to appear competent and trustworthy and be able to handle any crisis that arises. We have been taught that the family liaison is just that—a liaison for the family—not a therapist, friend, or family member. Compassion is the most important quality we could possess in doing our jobs here. Each of us must be able to determine what specific needs exist within the family in order to bring them to the company's attention.

If a need is unreasonable or cannot be met, we will have to find a way to communicate in a delicate manner why it can't be met. We may also be responsible for asking sensitive and uncomfortable questions that will lead to the eventual identification of the family's loved one, and during this conversation, the art of communication is critical.

The families are not allowed in the command center. It is an area cordoned off for Emergency Response Team employees where sensitive information is shared. The team has been instructed to keep the families on the lower levels of the hotel, and we take turns manning the elevators throughout the day to check badges and make certain no one who is unauthorized can approach the room.

When dealing with a family member, the team members will use the tactics learned in training for effective communication, beginning with the process of mirroring. Mirroring entails analyzing the family member's body language, tone of voice, and word usage, to determine how best to respond. If a family member sits down, we should also be seated, so that we may converse with them at eye level. This way, eye contact would be achieved in a nonthreatening manner, encouraging an open flow of communication. If the family member uses hushed tones, we are to respond the same way, versus loud tones that the individual may not be accustomed to. Mirroring is a process of following the lead and communication signals of an individual we do not know well but need to effectively respond to in order to achieve a specific goal. If we can make the family member feel comfortable, he or she is far more likely to open up and it will be easier to establish a bond. If the person the family has designated as their spokesman does not connect well with the individual the airline has assigned to them, the family is likely to have a bad feeling for the airline after everything is over. The airline has carefully planned this.

I am huddled with six others at a table when a commotion takes over the front of the room.

"*Bastardos!*"

Shouts come from the hallway and the door to the command center suddenly flies open. Two large men wearing dark suits shove their way in. The door strikes a woman standing there, sending the papers she had in her arms to the floor. She stumbles backwards and John North races to the door, pushing it closed.

"*Bastardos! Donde' esta' mi hijo usted los bastardos!*" Bastards, what have you done with my son, you bastards?

The men push harder and the door caves in.

"Someone help me here!" John shouts, and three other men in the room rush over, thrusting their bodies against the door in a human barricade. George Jones walks over, pulling John aside. They talk for several moments.

"Stay calm," a man at the table tells us. "Let's continue about our business."

We continue to work organizing files, but the commotion continues.

"He wants to know where his son is," Barbara says. "Apparently it's the only body we haven't found."

"I hope that's not the guy from the drug cartel," a man at the table whispers.

We watch as George Jones straightens his jacket and opens the door quickly, stepping outside. Three of our people accompany him into the hallway to confront the two angry men. George will talk to them in the way we have been trained to, using methods and skills to diffuse their concerns until there can be a conclusion. My chest tightens. I am sad for the father because we've done everything we can. Nothing we say can console him or change what has occurred.

# chapter eleven

# Communication

The days are a blur. I have lost all track of the calendar the way one does on an extended vacation. I have been in Cali for three days, though it feels like much longer. The most astounding fact thus far is that so much of what we have accomplished here has been far beyond anything that was talked about in training. Many of us have made several trips back and forth to the airport, and others have worked to prepare confidential documentation on passenger remains. We had been warned to be flexible and spontaneous, and I suppose this is what they meant.

I have seen several members of my team already, recognizing them by the names on their badges, but we have all been too busy to connect. Most arrived in the middle of the night from different destinations and have already been ferried out to various points throughout the city. Occasionally we pass in the lobby, as we escort family members around the hotel, navigating them from one room to the next until additional updates on their loved ones can be obtained. Employees fluent in Spanish have been used as interpreters on the ground, translating the interactions between our senior executives and local officials in meetings and in the transfer of written communication. Others have been sent on daily car runs for supplies and documentation.

Committing our actions and thoughts about specific passengers to paper during the activation is discouraged, because it is possible that the records could be subpoenaed if any lawsuit occurred. We want to do what's best for the families first and foremost and we have been told to ask ourselves: Should I be committing this to paper? Should I be making copies? Like any other smart corporation, the crisis response plan has been carefully thought out and executed. I write nothing down while I'm working in the administrative role at the command center. The files on the family members are confidential and it is imperative during this time that sensitive information does not get back to the families, or transmitted to the media. I pray that more will be found alive, but the numbers stream in by the hour and the count brings despair. At this point I have heard so much that I don't know what to think or feel. My body has moved into automatic, and when I gauge my feelings, I am numb. I am not tired, nor hungry, nor happy, nor sad. I am no longer euphoric at the possibility that a survivor will be found, I am only focused on the job in front of me.

On the ground, rescue workers report the grim statistics by radio and updates arrive at the command center by the hour. The death toll is high and there have been no more survivors. In most aviation accidents, the pilots' bodies are the most important to investigators early in the investigation because a medical examination can help rule out causes of the crash. Investigators will determine if the pilot had any preexisting diseases that could be responsible for a sudden incapacitation, such as an aorta rupture, kidney stones, or asthmatic attacks, but this wouldn't lead to anything conclusive since the flight had a copilot as well. Injury patterns of the hands and feet might be used to identify who was in control of the aircraft, and fractures of the hands might exist if the pilot had been holding the wheel or stick during the crash sequence. All of the findings combined determine the reason the plane went down.

Investigators at the morgue will work in the next few days to gather specimens to conduct the standard screening for drugs, both illegal and therapeutic, and alcohol. If evidence of drugs is found in the urine or blood, the tissue samples will be tested to determine if the concentrations present could have had adverse effects. If the bodies test positive for alcohol, it will have to be determined how much was ingested, or even if the alcohol was consumed at all, since alcohol becomes present in tissues as a natural part of the decomposition process. It's a standard procedure in any crash, used to rule out the various causes of the accident as quickly as possible.

In the evening, my hotel room is empty, and I decide to take advantage of the time alone by running water for a hot bath. The bathroom is constructed mainly of wood, with a cherry finish and elaborate Spanish tiles surrounding the sink and walls. As the suds envelop my body, I trace my fingers along the hand-crafted tub tiles, a remarkably intricate series of cobalt panels etched with images of birds and flowers. The doors leading out of the bathroom are arched to duplicate the architecture of the rest of the hotel, which is reminiscent of a European monastery.

In the courtyard outside the bathroom window, a massive oak commands the attention of hotel guests who pause to take pictures or sip coffee beneath its colossal branches. From my vantage point in the tub, I can see the tree, and I lean back in the water and examine the limbs that seem to reach out for the sky.

Everything has happened so fast. The training class, the crash, the call. Three pivotal events even by themselves, but now they are connected. The training had been followed by a plane crash, the crash had been followed by the call. The call had come in the dead of night, launching me into a world I wasn't even certain I wanted to experience.

But the call had been placed, and I had answered it, along with the others on the team. And now that I'm here I wonder, why would they want to join an Emergency Response Team? Why would anyone subject themselves to trauma, when trauma is the one thing we all wish to escape?

I ponder this question, because the psychological aspect of such a decision intrigues me, though I have not yet figured out the answer for myself. Why did I sign up for this program? *Because I never gave thought to the consequence,* I decide. From the very first phone call we had received notifying each of us of the crash, there was no turning back. We would be altered forever, and from that moment on we would be making the calls and continuing the domino effect that would launch strangers into a world that would forever change their lives.

# chapter twelve

# Ante Mortem

"When speaking with the family members you've been assigned to, do not use the word 'crash.' Use the terms 'incident,' 'accident,' or 'event,' to refer to what happened," the instructor had said.

From that point on, each of us had taken to using the word "incident" in the training class when referring to an airplane crash. Part of the preparation we had been given included role-plays that would prepare us for the initial phone call and any additional contact with a family. If the role-play involved calling a family to notify them of a major airplane crash, none of us uttered the word "crash." "Incident," I would say in training, overemphasizing every syllable. I understood the meaning behind finding a neutral word to diffuse the tragedy, but "incident" seemed far too trivial.

On day two of training, we had learned that family contact would include telephone calls and face-to-face meetings, which would only occur if we were assigned to a victim's loved ones. If a face-to-face meeting with a family occurred, it would most likely entail an ante mortem, the methodical process of identifying a victim. Ante mortem is a term that means "before death," and is a process in which a worksheet is used to gather physical identifying information about the crash victim. The document is five to six pages in length and contains a long list of intrusive questions that are hard for me to imagine asking. Did your wife have breast implants? Did your mother have any tattoos? What kind of jewelry was your grandmother wearing that day? What color and brand underwear did your husband wear?

The ante mortem process is uncomfortable, but it is a vital tool in speeding up the identification of the victims. Knowing specific physical details about an individual helps investigators and medical staff match the physical descriptions provided by the family to the remains found at the crash site. It's unpleasant for everyone involved, but for some families, it triggers the acceptance and finality of losing their loved one.

For others, the ante mortem results in a surge of anger against the Emergency Response Team member asking the questions. In class, we were warned to prepare for this and to look for certain signs that the anger is escalating out of control by monitoring specific body language and verbal cues. We were told to stay in tune to the person's feelings about the process. In the past, team members faced with a violent outburst had quickly called the command center for rescue. In training, we were given a specific code word to use in case the same thing should happen.

Here in Cali, our team will facilitate the identification process using ante mortems and any other methods possible, including DNA. The questions need to be asked gently, yet forcefully, to get the answers that would help investigators match specific physical details to a passenger's remains.

We have all been trained on this process, and the instructor had divided us into small groups in a role-play scenario in which each one of us would attempt to gain the vital information needed in order to identify a body. One of us would act as the Emergency Response Team member and the other would play the part of the grieving family member until everyone had acted out the scene. It was an exercise that would be graded by the class and evaluated by the instructors, who would use it to determine who possessed the communication skills to serve as a family liaison and who did not. For some, the exercise meant the difference between making the team or being removed from the list of candidates. We had been given just fifteen minutes to prepare.

When the assignments had been handed out, my role was that of an Emergency Response Team member meeting a family for the first time in their own home. I would have to probe deeply for the answers to a laundry list of uncomfortable questions and at the end of the role-play the class would determine if I had achieved the ultimate goal: compiling the information needed from the ante mortem document to identify the body of a passenger.

During my fifteen minutes of preparation, I decided it would help if I wrote a few pages on how I thought the ante mortem would go. As a child, I learned to use writing to work through my problems by writing long passages about the day I would be reunited with my father, writing poems to him, and filling journals with paragraphs about what I would say the moment I first saw him. In my teenage years, my writing turned angrier, but I used pen and paper to vent all of it, writing the poetry and dark stories that reflected my hardened heart. Writing had become an outlet for me to prepare for a major event, and this one was easy to envision.

*I knew when I approached the Martin house that this would be the toughest day of my life. I had never met Mr. Martin, but it was to be his most difficult day as well, and our lives would forever be bound together by this moment. I rehearsed my lines as I walked up the carefully manicured sidewalk leading to the Victorian-style house in Darien. Driving into the New England suburb from the chaos of the city was like entering another world. The old houses were beautifully appointed, each taking on a character of its own like a wise old woman who has witnessed many generations and a lifetime of change pass before her. The Martin house was covered in vines and stood high on a grassy hill scattered with Appalachian pine trees. I pictured the children playing in the side yard on the trampoline that was visible from*

*the street, the trampoline that stood empty now, an unwelcome
reminder of five-year-old Morgan and ten-year-old Michael. I rang the
bell and he answered immediately.*

"Hello, Mr. Martin?"

According to the assignment, I would offer my hand but he would
not take it. I would have to enter the house and ask him if I could sit
down. We had all learned in training that if you ask to be seated, the
victim's family members usually sit down with you, which creates a
relaxed atmosphere conducive for delivering the message. But in the
role-play to which I was assigned, the family member is still in shock,
and he refuses to sit down. Mr. Martin is a middle-aged executive.
He was the provider of his family, and now he's alone.

*He is a strong, solid man in his early fifties with the bronzed
appearance of an actor in a golf-resort commercial. He steadies himself against a heavy mahogany chair in the living room, looking tired
and drawn as if he hadn't slept the night before. I decide against sitting and stand there on the hardwood floor, the chair between us.
Around the room are reminders of the life he'd created for them.
Shades of hunter green and burgundy decorate the den and the hand-
carved bookshelves overflow with leather-bound books on various sub-
jects. Faulkner, Tolstoy, and Dr. Seuss, mixed with picture books on
Europe and the Caribbean. I know from their flight records that they
were well-traveled and had flown over three million miles together,
earning the airline's Elite Club status for frequent flyers. I also knew
that they seldom traveled apart. Three million miles without incident,
and now this.*

*Toys lay scattered about in their living room and a Curious George
doll like the one I had when I was a child sat alone in an easy chair. The
warmth of family vacation photos and soft scent of potpourri lingered in
the air. A woman's touch. A constant reminder of the wife he now does
not have, the wife that he had just a day ago, the wife whose youthful
smile haunts me from behind a beveled picture frame on a table just
beyond where her husband is standing. I try to get right to the point.*

When it was my turn for the exercise, I brought my notes to the front of the room and glanced at them briefly before making eye contact with the other actor, playing the man who has lost his wife. My words were direct and clear.

"Mr. Martin, we've confirmed that your wife and children were indeed on the airplane. We've verified the passenger list from the flight and all three of them made the connection in Atlanta to Flight 451, the airplane that went down yesterday."

The actor Mr. Martin remained expressionless and clung to the back of the chair like a valiant soldier. According to the assignment, he does not resist. Instead, he does something we must always be prepared for. He reacts with denial, insisting that he has just spoken with his family. His wife and two kids had called from the Atlanta airport where they were making their connection to the fateful flight, and he had talked with them. But he does not acknowledge that they boarded the ill-fated airplane. Mr. Martin was in shock and could not fathom the reality that his entire family had died in the crash.

"Mr. Martin, I'll need to ask you a few questions in order for our team to obtain a positive identification of your family so we can get them back home for the funeral arrangements."

I was professional and calm, but halfway through the role-play I realized that Mr. Martin the actor had tears streaming down his face. A knot formed in my throat, and I held it there. It was a single role-play, not even real, yet I felt an overwhelming sadness and my eyes welled. I felt sad for Mr. Martin, but also sad for myself, and for everyone else in the world who had ever experienced something tragic. It was a moment where one sad thing triggers the memory of another. Instead of grieving for the situation in front of you, you grieve for every bad thing that has ever happened.

*Do not cry. Do not cry. Do not cry*, I repeated silently, trying to force these terrible thoughts from my head. *Do not cry, you idiot*, I said, sternly berating myself until the knot disappeared. I could do this. I could be strong for others and complete all the tests involved to become a member of the Emergency Response Team so I could make a difference in someone else's life.

In Cali, it is at the command center on the seventh day after the crash when I remember the role-play. Now I am in the midst of hundreds of Mr. Martins, and it is all so real.

# chapter thirteen

# Jim Johnson

When I first meet Julie, it is the third full day since my arrival in Cali. It's after ten in the evening when she walks into the hotel room, her arms filled with paper bags from the grocer. She has brought back bottles of water, a toothbrush, and incidentals from the local pharmacy. She is a thin girl and her hair is conservatively styled. She wears a navy-blue skirt and jacket with matching navy pumps and a company pin with the airplane logo affixed to her lapel. I help her with the bags.

"Hello, I'm Tammy. I assume you're my roommate?"

"Yes...Julie Davis. Nice to meet you."

Her hand is cold, but she is professional, prepared, and everything we are expected to be. I had been told during the hiring process that only those with the right *profile* would be chosen to represent the airline in front of corporate America, and with one glance I can see that Julie fits. Her hair is neat, her suit tailored so that the skirt falls just below the knee. Like everyone else, she has passed a series of stringent tests just to get hired.

Julie lowers herself onto the bed and removes her jacket. She stays busy while we talk, removing more clothes from her suitcase and folding them into neat squares, folding the T-shirts first, then the underwear. She does this methodically, placing them in a drawer of the armoire.

Her career path has been a lot like mine, except that she is ten years older, far more seasoned, and African-American. We have both received reams of corporate training over the years, but there are differences as well. Julie is single, has an advanced degree in marketing, and comes from a large family. When I ask her why she has joined the Emergency Response Team, she explains that she's on the executive fast track, a special program to groom executives for advancement.

"The ERT is a requirement if I want to advance my career," she says, pulling a large black notebook from her suitcase. Inside are several tabs of information containing the series of steps required before graduation from the executive program. Upon graduation, the executives are moved into high-level management jobs within other organizations.

"But why would they groom you only to have you move out of the airline? That doesn't make sense."

She sighs and looks at me as if she has something more to say. Eventually she turns away, moving to the closet to hang up her jacket.

I wonder if it's a program to advance minorities within the company, or if it's just some standout executive program I'm not aware of because I haven't achieved enough to qualify for it. Julie is two levels higher than I am within the company, and within the year, she explains, she will be moved to her new position within another corporation, a major bank in Houston. She has worked a crash activation before, but this is her last.

"The last one was enough for me," Julie says. "But when I was called for this one I decided to take it. I know it will be good on my résumé. I'm sure they'll give me a major role here."

"I noticed a few suits in your closet," I say. "I didn't bring one."

"You'll need one."

"What for?"

"You should always travel with a navy-blue blazer because you never know who you'll meet or what your assignment will be. Didn't they tell you that?"

"No."

"If you're assigned to work with a family you'll need to look professional. You're the face of the airline. The one representative they will have the most contact with."

"I'm not sure what my assignment is yet."

"Each day it'll be different, but chances are you'll get a family."

"Do you have one?" I ask.

"No, I won't take one. I don't want that assignment."

"Why not?"

"You can borrow my jacket," she says, ignoring the question. She moves from the bed to the closet and pulls out a simple navy-blue blazer. I take it and try it on. It fits perfectly.

"Thanks. But are you sure?"

"Yes, I've got others. You should wear it every day, even to the command center. When you're walking through the lobby, the reporters will see you, and so will everyone else. Better to look too professional than not professional enough. And as a woman, you can't make the mistake of looking too informal. You're judged by the way you dress and act, and if you have to perform an ante mortem, you'll need to look authoritative."

"Have you ever performed one?"

"Several. It's one of the hardest things you'll do."

She resumes putting the clothes away until her two drawers are filled.

"Just be sure to follow the rules," she says. "Be careful about everything you say and be careful about not leaving your notes lying around. Once this is all over and the cause of the crash is determined, it gets crazy. You don't want to be in a position to be subpoenaed by a family's attorney for something you said to them during this process."

"What do you mean? I don't follow."

"People have been subpoenaed in the past for things they've mentioned about the cause of the crash, for instance, or relaying information to the family that the family has turned around and used against the airline. If that happens, your career is over. You have to be responsible, even when you hear others speculating."

I nod my head, remembering the words of the executive who had called to deliver the news that I'd been hired.

*This industry isn't easy*, he had warned. *I'm taking a big risk by hiring you straight out of college with no management experience, so I'm counting on you to go places.*

I had no intention of letting him down. I was certain I could handle the task ahead and anything that was handed to me. I knew enough to know that when in a public place, I should not talk about the crash or any aspect of the activation in order to be sensitive to any family members who might be present.

In the morning, Julie and I wait at the curb in front of the hotel for a taxi. The moon lingers ominously in a magnificent white ball to invite the day, and it occurs to me that even with the poverty and despair, Latin America holds a visitor captive in its charms. It is a place beyond beautiful, a place where at times it seems impossible to be poor.

In some parts, like Machu Picchu, the rain falls in perfume drops, and all across the country the street children beg for money with false sadness, approaching the tourist with a fixed frown. They plead for help, reciting pop culture and factoids about America in hopes it will bring in a dollar. They know the nation's capitol, the name of the president, and a handful of famous actors. They are tiny little salesmen, and when the dollar is firm in their grip you can witness the playful smile appear until the next tourist comes along. But this morning I have prepared for them, so when Julie and I are approached, I have candy from the mini-bar and a bag of chips. The boy approaches with the sad frown, grabs the offering, and runs away, ripping the chip bag open at once. The taxi arrives and as I climb inside I look back to see the boy sharing the candy I have given him with the other street children.

The drive to the Intercontinental Hotel is a brief fifteen minutes and we head directly to the command center. I go to the bulletin board that contains the list with our assignments for the day. A small crowd has gathered there. Some have been up all night—they are easy to spot with their bloodshot eyes and creased clothes. I am grateful for the sleep I've had so far and the fact that I have not been given an assignment to work through the night. But I also realize that my time will come.

I locate my name halfway down the list and see the word "airport" beside it. I move to the table where the assignment crew is working and find Jason, the young man who met my arrival on the first day.

"Excuse me," I interrupt.

He closes the file folder he's perusing and I offer him my hand.

"What can I help you with today? Did you need your assignment file?" He glances at my name tag and thumbs through a file box without hesitation until he finds a folder with my last name stenciled on the tab.

"Here," he says, handing it to me. He pulls the folder back and peeks inside. "Wait a minute, let me see where they've got you." He reads through it and then hands it to me.

"Looks like the airport. You're going this morning to pick up a box of hairbrushes that have arrived from the states. They'll be in the general manager's office, which is just behind the ticket counter."

"Hairbrushes?"

"Yeah, for DNA. We ask the families to send them to help identify the passengers."

When an airplane goes down and the death toll is high, the first order of business on the ground is to establish a makeshift morgue where the bodies of the passengers will be transported for the process of identification. The makeshift morgue our workers have established is in close proximity to the crash site, and each day the bodies had come in for the process of identification. In the United States, refrigerated trucks would be used to transport the remains of passengers from the wreckage to the morgue, but here there are none, and the terrain at the crash site is so unpredictable that standard cars cannot traverse it. The military has been brought in to assist our team, and when a Jim Johnson is located, he or she is transported immediately from the wreckage in the easiest and most efficient manner possible.

Tissue samples are taken or DNA and medical records are requested from the families, so that the intensive process of identification can occur. As with all fatal airline crashes, DNA will be used here as the foremost technique for identifying passengers and eliminating options regarding the cause of crash. Biological tissues such as saliva, skin, blood, or hair will be examined.

I leave Jason at the table and find the guy with the car keys, who will also give me directions. He draws me a crude map to the airport and warns me about the smash and grab, a crime where drivers and passengers are accosted in their cars by men who smash in the car window to grab watches and necklaces. The airport isn't far from the command hotel, but getting lost is not an option in this country, which is known for kidnappings, drug trafficking, and terrorism. In the hotel parking lot, I find the car quickly by the license tag he has written down on a tiny slip of paper. The car resembles all the others, small and nondescript, with tiny tires.

The drive is twenty-five kilometers, but it is a straight shot down several city streets. I turn on a road a mile from the airport and come to a complete stop, counting fifteen cars in the line ahead of me. At a crossroads, a procession of cars pass through flanked by military cars with sirens. It looks like a funeral procession, but I cannot be sure. On the dirt shoulder beside the traffic, several old women lurch forward, walking slowly with packs of supplies loaded on their backs. I stare out the window too long and one of them approaches my car, her eyes distressing and far away. She says something in Spanish that I cannot understand, but I lean over and toss out some pesos before pulling away. In the rearview mirror, I can see her doing the same thing to the next car, but the driver ignores her and accelerates.

Inside the Cali airport, I find the airline ticket counter easily because it's far nicer and cleaner than the others. The American-based carriers are sometimes resented for the money they bring in, which far surpasses the capital the local carriers have. But America has been good for Colombia, and any Colombian who can get a job with a United States carrier has a chance to eventually find work in the United States.

I identify myself to a female agent at the counter, a Colombian woman who does not return my smile. She speaks to me in Spanish, and when I cannot understand she shakes her head as if I'm the stupidest person she has ever met and escorts me to a room in the back. She says something in Spanish to the agent sitting there, an older woman working on an outdated computer. The woman rises from her computer, lifting a finger in the air that signals me to wait. They disappear to a room in the back and return minutes later, carrying a large mail pouch.

"Here it is," says the agent, handing me a bulky shipping envelope. "This is what you need."

"*Gracias*," I reply.

The envelope is heavy and feels as if it contains ten or twelve brushes in different sizes. I place it in the backseat of my vehicle and secure it with a seatbelt. As I drive away, I check the rearview mirror and watch the airport shrink behind me, imagining all of the relatives who left the terminal that day without the passengers they had intended to pick up. On the way to the airport their hearts had been full and without worry, yet the drive home was very different, a drive filled with despair and confusion. It is a thought that makes my heart heavy. In my back seat I have the hairbrushes of dead people, people who just days before had been passengers on a jet, humans with individual lives and dreams. I become aware of the enormity of the package that is on the seat behind me. *I am carrying the DNA of the dead*, DNA that will identify each one so that we can send them in a Jim Johnson box to their families.

People survive in more than 80 percent of all plane crashes, but this crash is not one of them. The death count is over a hundred already. The captain will return as a Jim Johnson, like hundreds of others, and at the crash site we will be able to soft-ID some of the passengers by a driver's license or document found in a wallet. Then investigators will try for a hard-ID utilizing genetics, such as fingerprinting. In previous crashes, anthropology tables have been used to measure the bones and then match them to their male or female counterpart.

The hairbrushes in the backseat will bring closure to several families. I imagine the owner of one of them, and as my mind drifts I can see her there at the mirror in her bathroom, cosmetics splayed across the sink. She is brushing her long, silken hair. She is vibrant and beautiful, with a life that has been a canvas of abstract strokes. She has had love, and lost love, she has been to school, smoked a cigarette, and has experienced the passion of waking beside a new lover in the middle of the night. She has tasted the sweetness of fresh apples in a warm apple pie, ridden horseback through a field, and experienced the birth of her child. Her days are a palette of colorful paints and she is the artist, with the brush firmly in her grip. She has lived through the change and growth that most of us experience on earth.

I can see her and feel her, and it is as if she is whispering in my ear. *But what is it all for?* The canvas that would contain her life is now empty, the future meaningless and bare. The end has come and there is no more tomorrow. She has died with a plane full of strangers, without the luxury of holding her child one last time. She will travel home as another Jim Johnson.

*  *  *

In the lobby of the command-center hotel, the families gather like robots. Some have already flown back home, but the ones who remain stay in their own silent worlds most of the time, despite the onslaught of activity. I move through the lobby towards the hotel ballroom, where I find Hector, my team member from Miami. He was the first team member I had called, and his assignment had been to escort a family from Miami to the hotel and then walk them through the process of identifying the passenger that belongs to them.

The other members of my team have been given various jobs; some have been sent to the homes of family members, some to the airport. The command center in Dallas has assigned Hector to a local family because of his Hispanic heritage and his ability to communicate with them in a sensitive manner. So far everything has gone well, despite the fact that a positive identification on their son was lurking around the corner. They had insisted on traveling to the crash site, and tomorrow, Hector would escort them there.

Hector is short and compact and wears a cross around his neck. There is a comfort about him, as if he could handle any situation with self-assurance. He makes a fine Emergency Response Team member, I think, because he can make anyone feel at ease.

At the entry to the ballroom, we encounter a reporter from the United States, amidst a congregation of family members. We cannot make them avoid the press. We can only discourage the press from confronting them.

"Will there be any additional survivors?" the reporter asks.

We continue walking, ignoring him. Everyone wants the answer to that question, but by now it is too late to believe there can be any more miracles. After the initial impact of most plane crashes, no matter how severe, there are passengers found alive in the wreckage. They may be found dangling from a seatbelt, staring out of a gaping hole in the aircraft, or trapped under a seat, but remarkably, they have survived. This crash is no exception, because even though the airplane has hurtled into the earth at high speed, four have managed to survive it. Reporters have managed to interview members of their families, who have kept a constant vigil at the hospital. Mauricio

Reyes, the college student from Michigan, recalled the memories of the flight to his family, describing a violent shaking inside the aircraft just seconds before the plane came to rest on the mountain. Instinctively, he had grabbed the hand of the girl sitting next to him, clutching it tight. It was Mercedes Ramirez, and hours later he found himself sprawled beside her on the ground, bleeding and injured.

I have found this to be one of the basic truths and mysteries of humanity. The human body can survive the most horrendous circumstances. Most of the passengers on the airplane died from the immediate impact of the plane hitting the mountain at full speed, yet against anyone's expectations, four humans walked out. They have survived the unimaginable, and now it seems as if they can survive anything that life hands them.

In my opinion, I doubt we will find any other survivors, because our rescue crew has been on the ground at the crash site for nine days and nights, in search of a sound, or a voice. Within seconds after an impact, the chance of survival decreases as smoke and fire engulf any part of the fuselage that is still intact. Hector and I have debated this point because he is a deeply religious man with an unshakable faith, and he believes there will be more survivors. In our quiet conversations away from the others, I tell him why I believe there will be no more. It has been too long since the plane went down. More than a week, and anyone who had a chance of surviving would have been found already.

He knows this deep in his heart because we have been taught that when the airplane comes to rest after an impact, the passengers have critical seconds to fight their way to exits, and even then the chances are limited because the environment will be unpredictable. The act of evacuating the aircraft can be as deadly as the plane crash itself because the air is filled with smoke, fire, and confusion, making the situation hazardous on every level. The ground is soaked with jet fuel, and carbon monoxide can seep into the fuselage, taking its victims silently by depriving vital organs of oxygen.

At the morgue, recovery efforts are in full swing. Because the airplane wasn't located until twelve hours after impact, rumors have surfaced about the possibility that guerrillas somehow contributed to the crash and hid the crash site from authorities. Although no one officially believes this to be true, the reports continue to come in, and experts across the nation hypothesize on the length of time that elapsed and whether or not more survivors could have been rescued.

Although it is obvious that most passengers perished from the impact itself, an official cause of death must accompany a death certificate.

Scientific studies on toxins have determined that if just ten percent of carboxyhemoglobin (COHb), the substance produced by carbon-monoxide exposure, were present in an individual's bloodstream, there would be no recognizable symptoms. Heavy smokers can have as much as 9 percent of the toxin in their system and still function normally. At a level of 15 percent, a passenger attempting to get out of a smoky fuselage might experience a mild headache, but nothing more. At 25 percent, the symptoms would include nausea and a serious headache, but the individual would still be able to function properly. At this level of exposure, the victim would experience a relatively quick recovery after treatment with oxygen or fresh air. But after even more time trapped in a smoky fuselage or assisting other passengers, the symptoms intensify, and when the toxin in the bloodstream reaches 30 percent, the potential for long-term effects increases. At 45 percent, the individual will usually experience unconsciousness, and at 55 percent or higher, the person will die.

*  *  *

Around the morgue, looters have been detained, and large trucks and buses have been strategically positioned outside the perimeter of the building to block any visibility from cameras or helicopters. I am grateful I will never have to go.

The worst possible has already happened. Team members at our Cali command center have received word that the body of a passenger has been stolen and a local group is demanding a cash payment to return it. The airline from America has money and the poverty in this country has made a group of local men do the unthinkable. At the crash site, our Emergency Response Team staff has witnessed other atrocities, one in which a young man was confronted trying on the pants of one of the victims, a scene that was followed by screaming and a foot chase. The man got away with the pants, and another boy was seen removing watches and rings from bodies.

Inside the morgue, pathologists and forensic experts from around the world perform victim identifications. I do not envy Hector, who will have to experience the trauma of it. The airplane is in small pieces and debris is scattered across the ground. Most everyone has assumed that the deaths have occurred from the initial impact as the airplane deconstructed, but the medical team will work through the nights until every passenger has been officially identified. The process of identification will be far more complex than a traditional autopsy investigation due to the nature of the injuries, but by the time we all leave here, every passenger should be named.

Hector and I find each other whenever we can to share words of encouragement, but when he is with his family, I do not talk to him. He has worked two crashes before this one, and the what-ifs still haunt him, though it is impossible to make sense of the what-ifs and turn back time.

When I see Hector the following morning, he has positively identified his family's son, but he has nothing to say. He cannot talk about it, and when he tries the tears well up in his eyes and he chokes on his words.

"All I can say is that it is the hardest thing I will ever do in my life." It is something I had already assumed, but I can see in his eyes that it was far worse than anything he imagined.

"If you need to talk about it, Hector, I'm here. Just let me know."

"Thanks. Did you hear about the report on the pilots?" he asks. "The cause of death has officially been determined to be blunt force trauma for the captain and the first officer. Also, they've sent specimens of the liver and blood to the local institute of medicine to be analyzed."

Blunt trauma simply means that the pilots died from the force of the impact like most of the other passengers. Specimen samples were standard after a crash, because the results would be noted in the investigative report and were important in determining the pilot's physical condition while operating the aircraft.

"Yes?" I say. "What did they find?"

"The samples from the body of the first officer were found to be negative for alcohol or drugs, but...the blood and liver samples from the captain were found to be positive."

"Positive? Meaning he was drinking or taking drugs?"

"Not necessarily. The tests were positive for alcohol and negative for drugs. We're sending samples from both bodies on a flight to the United States, to the forensic toxicology laboratory at the Armed Forces Institute of Pathology. I guess we'll know more then."

I imagine that once the news of this gets out, the press will have every paper filled with articles speculating about the condition of our pilots. As much as I like Hector and respect him for his beliefs and integrity, I cannot be sure of anything until we get home and the dust has settled. And until the full investigation has been completed, I'm determined not to believe or even contemplate the cause of the crash. No one knows the cause at this point, and it's possible that even the pilots themselves had no idea what had happened.

# chapter fourteen

# The Investigation Continues

It has been nine days since the airplane went down. At the command center, a woman I have not yet been introduced to hands out copies of a press release asking each of us to read through it. Each day there are several new faces, most of whom pass by once and then disappear. The assignments vary from minute to minute, and each day we are placed with different members of the team or given tasks to complete on our own.

The topic of the morning is the cockpit voice recorder, also known as the CVR, which has been located and shipped to the National Transportation Safety Board. Below us the reporters swarm the lobby, all of them wanting a comment on the contents of the voice box.

The press release is on official stationery and has been drafted by the local governing body of aviation, with the assistance of the airline and airplane manufacturer. It has been sent to local media organizations and to media across the world, outlining the details of the crash in a concise, factual manner that cannot be construed to pinpoint blame. I read the release quickly:

*Flight 965 was a regularly scheduled passenger flight with one hundred fifty-five passengers and eight crewmembers aboard. The airplane crashed into mountainous terrain during a descent under*

*instrument flight rules. Four passengers survived. The flight made ini-*
*tial radio contact with the approach control personnel while descend-*
*ing to a flight level of twenty thousand feet. It was then cleared to*
*descend, and the pilots were told that no delay was expected for the*
*approach.*

The woman explains that the investigative team has successfully
downloaded the data from the flight data recorder for the final thirty
minutes of flight. The cockpit voice recorder has been transcribed
and the quality is good. So far the data shows that there was a normal, extended conversation among the cockpit flight crew prior to
descent, conversation about the job, other pilots, and the landing.
There is no indication of descent checklist procedures, however, and
no indication of an approach-procedures briefing. There is also no
indication of any aircraft-system malfunction, or any unusual mete-
orological event, such as turbulence or wind shear.

The cockpit voice recorder has ruled out the presence of an
external hostile force on the aircraft, such as a terrorist. Everything
that can be heard on the recorder has been analyzed using technical devices to determine if there are sounds other than voices. An
explosion caused by a bomb would be clearly audible on a cockpit
recorder and has been in previous crashes with other airlines. But
in this crash there is no indication of any problem, nor anything
out of the ordinary related to the ground-based navigational aids.
The cockpit recorder showed that radio communications were
accomplished from the left seat of the cockpit, and that there was
no evidence of language difficulty by either the flight crew or the
air-traffic controller. The flight had been operating in a radar sur-
veillance environment until a few minutes before the end of the
flight, when radar coverage was no longer available. This is all the
information she has and it is all the information that will be
released to the press. A statement at the bottom of the release suggests that all media requests be forwarded to the local civil aviation
authority in Colombia.

The Global Positioning System data stored in the flight data recorder will be studied to determine positioning relative to major landmarks, which could offer evidence involving wind shear or weather mishaps. After that, a full reconstruction of the crash can be completed after reviewing all the data on engine state, cockpit conversation and action, weather variables, and surface position. The data contained within the flight data recorder and cockpit voice recorders are usually enough to ascertain the cause of the crash, but the contents of the voice recorder will be strictly controlled. The information may be sensitive and the pilots may have had last words that the public should not hear. To protect their privacy, we will keep the data under the highest security until a transcript of the initial half-hour leading up to the crash is produced.

Several men in FBI jackets have congregated in the hotel lobby. They are there to investigate the possibility of terrorist activity and any other attack that would have caused the airplane to crash. Julie's assignment for the day is to shuttle them back and forth to various spots across the city, including the airport.

The most interesting thing that's occurred this morning involves a team member who has been assigned the precarious task of keeping two women apart during their stay in Cali, who have both turned out to be the fiancées of the same victim. She must call them in their rooms and tell each of them she will be at their door to escort them to the hotel lobby for breakfast. The women had flown in from the United States last night, yet neither is aware of the other. Our task is to separate the women at different tables in the lobby restaurant, seating them far enough apart so that conflict is avoided. At the command center, the team member corners me and asks if I'll help.

"Just be a decoy for a little while in the lobby," she says. "Let me get the other one situated at a table."

Their loved one was a young man from Milwaukee who left behind a life of loose ends.

Both women had called the airline after seeing the reports of the airplane crash on the news, and both had known he had taken the flight to Latin America that day. He had given them his social security number and things only a fiancée or loved one would know. There was no way we could refuse travel to one and not the other. Emergency Response Team members at airline headquarters had spoken to several family members who confirmed that one of them was indeed his fiancée, while other friends and family members assured us that the other girl was his fiancée. One of the girls has brought along a photo album and the other a framed picture that the victim had given her.

In the lobby, I wait by a pillar until the team member with fiancée number one passes, taking a seat in the hotel restaurant. It is a casual place with tables situated on a tile floor, and she finds one in the back, sheltered by three palms. After five minutes, the team member returns, just in time to find fiancée number two exiting the elevator. They walk over and she introduces us.

"Can you stay here a minute with Tammy?" she asks. "I'll get us a table."

"Sure," the girl says. Her demeanor is surprisingly even, and it does not seem like she has been crying, at least not today. She carries a scrapbook under her arm.

"Can I see your pictures?"

"Sure," she says, opening it slowly. We stand there and look through it, at images of her with a young man outdoors, standing by some trees, the same young man by a sports car, and the two of them playing with dogs. I notice a gold band with a tiny diamond chip on her left finger.

I wonder when the truth will come out, when the family and friends of the young man will finally be exposed to another side of him, the one they were not aware of. Will it come out during the funeral, when the two women are asked to perform eulogies? Or will it come out in a day, at the crash site, when they overhear a stranger from the airline talking about it? Maybe it will never come out at all. I feel strange being a part of his deception, continuing his legacy of lies.

The team member returns and takes the girl away and I decide to take a minute to clear my head. I find an empty chair in the far corner of the lobby where I sit and open my journal. I make a list of the loose ends that I would not want the world to see, things that would give a shadow impression but not the complete picture of who I am. Simple things like an invoice for a bounced check and things that are far more complex. I will update my will, I will clean out my closets, and I will get rid of anything I am not proud of. I will live as if the world is watching, as if it were my last day. I will live as I should have been living all along, as if God is watching my every move.

*   *   *

"Have you gotten your assignment yet today?" asks Julie.

"Not yet."

"Hope you're not getting a family. Why don't you ask George to keep you at the command center for the administrative tasks?"

"Maybe."

I say this but I have no intention of doing it. The administrative tasks are necessary, but the command center seems crowded with people and long lapses between activities. At times we are needed, but often the most we can do is sit around and speculate, about the rumors of the passengers, their lives, and the loose ends they have left behind.

Across the polished marble floors where I sit, a cluster of relatives from one family drape themselves over several chairs. Some sit on the floor and read, while others drink coffee and wait for information about their passenger. He was a forty-year-old executive who had traveled frequently to Colombia on business, but this is the first trip here for his aging parents, and his daughter and wife. They are holding up well, even though his body has been found in the wreckage and brought to the morgue. The possibility that he will ever return to them as a survivor is gone, yet they seem filled with peace and I watch them in awe. They laugh and tell stories. A large photograph of him sits in a chair all on its own. They have found their own closure and are celebrating his life, not mourning his death.

# chapter fifteen

# Milagro

The early-morning sun beams in through the windows in the lobby, illuminating the floor. I stand beside the door and peek inside the ball-room, where the mood is solemn and strangely quiet. There are no sobs and there are no protests, just shells of people waiting for the next step.

The family members have been issued tags that allow me to iden-tify who can enter and who cannot. I stand there for hours, until I can recognize them without looking at their tags anymore. They are fidgety and unpredictable, and they pace all day, back and forth, back and forth, in uncontrolled anxiety.

"Yo," a hand grabs my shoulder.

I turn to face Hector, who hands me a single sheet of paper that looks like some sort of shipping invoice.

"Special delivery!" he cracks a smile and kisses me on the cheek, as he does with everyone.

"How can you be so cheerful all the time?"

He pulls the wallet from his back pocket as he has done so many times before and flashes the photograph of his children.

"Hard to have a bad day with kids around," he says.

"So what's going on?"

"I have good news," he says, smiling. "We need to go to the airport."

"I don't understand…"

"They found a dog in the wreckage and she's alive! You and I need to go to the airport and pick up a dog carrier because hers was destroyed in the crash."

"You're kidding?" My heart rises. It is a small victory, but a victory nonetheless. It has been nine days since the plane went down, eight since the airplane and all the survivors were found. "What kind of dog?" I ask.

"She's a small brown mutt, some kind of mixed breed. Nobody has claimed her yet but the locals want her, our people want her, and so does the rescue worker who found it. They've named her Milagro."

"Milagro?"

"Spanish for 'miracle.' C'mon girl, you need to learn your Spanish."

There had been thousands of pounds of cargo in the cargo hold where Milagro was found, but somehow the dog had survived the crushing impact.

"Someone said she was found up in a tree," Hector added. "Imagine that, the little dog carrier all up in the tree branches."

\* \* \*

The drive to the airport is short and Hector takes a back road on the return to lengthen it. Outside, the sky is surprisingly vibrant and the streets filled with life, something I have forgotten. Life does exist, but it is outside the walls of the hotel. In the distance, towering beyond the straight road in front of me is the mountain range where the survivors were found. The jungle is usually quiet, but now it is an entirely different jungle of machines and people and foreigners invading the land. I cannot help but think of the four survivors, *four and a half* survivors, who have made it out. On previous trips to the jungle, I have waded knee-deep in the swamp, hunted alligators in a rickety canoe, and eaten piranha. I've pulled ticks from my arms and legs, extracted a scorpion from my shoe, and trekked two long miles on a solitary plank over ominous waters inhabited by anacondas. In the jungle, survival is possible, but survival bleeding and injured is a miracle, especially after twelve hours.

At the airport we learn from a staff member that Milagro was first spotted by a Colombian soldier from the army unit that had worked on the rescue mission. Milagro will be adopted by the army unit, it has been decided, and will stay in Colombia unless someone from his family comes forward to claim him. Although the dog's photograph has been displayed in the local papers and is well on its way to the United States press, no extended family member has come forth, and Milagro has remained grateful to his rescuers, offering licks and affection to anyone who will hold him.

Milagro's new carrier is tucked safely in the backseat of our car. Hector and I have talked a lot about miracles, and although the dog's name is appropriate, I do not understand yet why the dog and those four passengers were chosen to live, chosen for the miracle. I do not know if I believe in miracles, because I have not experienced any of my own. But I do know that one of the passengers had missed the connection that would have put her on Flight 965 that day, despite a frantic attempt to make it. When a reporter tracked her down after the crash, the woman said, "It's a miracle." But I wonder silently if it was a miracle at all, because all of those other people died. Every situation and circumstance is labeled depending upon our perception. For a survivor, the plane crash was a miracle. For a grieving family member, the plane crash was nothing more than a tragedy.

Hector and I pull into the packed hotel parking lot and find an empty spot directly in front of the door. Upstairs in the command center, Hector is given an assignment, and when I find Jason, I learn how I'll be spending the rest of my day.

"You have been assigned to a family," he announces, handing me a file. "Read up and head down to the ballroom. They've got name badges on."

I have spent days worrying about it, but I can escape it no longer. The file contains the profile of a middle-aged couple from New

Jersey who we have transported to Cali to complete the process of identifying their grown son, who had been traveling with his wife and children. One child, a son, had stayed behind, because they thought he was too young for the trip. The couple has been here for days, and we have found room for them in the command center hotel. We have tried to do everything right, but their luggage has been lost in the process and it still has not been found. It is a minor challenge. The loss of luggage compared to the larger loss they have suffered is insignificant. Nevertheless, the luggage must be located and it will be my job to make certain they are taken care of in the meantime.

"You'll need to get them some money to replace their clothing," Jason says. "You should probably request it as soon as possible after you introduce yourself."

The file suggests that my family will need the money and also a cell phone so they can communicate with their family in New Jersey. They will need almost two thousand dollars to replace clothing and incidentals for both of them, as well as any food they might want while they're here. The hotel has offered our staff cars, vans, and even their own personnel to help out when necessary, and if I need to, I can arrange for a trip to the store to buy clothing for my family.

I step into the elevator oblivious to the sounds around me. Three women enter, their nails long and pristine, gripping shopping bags stuffed with purchases. Their suits are expensive, and they are drenched in perfume that assaults my nostrils and causes me to step back. The elevator moves in slow motion, and it seems to me that we have stopped on every floor and the lobby is miles below. I know and yet do not comprehend that I am just reacting on autopilot, fear, and sleep deprivation. One of the women says something that the others find funny and they laugh. Inside I am enraged, and it is not until they exit on the fifth floor and I am left alone that I realize they are allowed to laugh. They are hotel guests, unrelated to the crash. They are not in my world.

In my world, the exuberance has passed and the curiosity is gone. I have seen so much already that I do not want to see more. Each morning, I see the relatives when I pass through the lobby where the walking dead linger and sit in small clusters so close together, but alone. Their eyes are blank and haunted, and the day has no purpose, except to wait. I have seen them at night and they look just the same. I emerge from the command center and move *through* them, like one passing the grotesquely disfigured or disabled—not wanting to ignore, yet not wanting to smile for fear that doing so will be taken the wrong way. The feeling is the same. I want to stop, acknowledge them, and offer warmth, but I am uncertain if the warmth will be received and if what I have to offer is even anything that they need.

The elevator door slides open and I step out into the noise of the lobby to the sounds of a reggae band. Near the front desk, a group of children shout, weaving in and out of a cluster of luggage. Large floral arrangements adorn the check-in desk and delivery cars arrive daily with more containing cards with the last name of the hotel guest. In the corner of the lobby, a television monitor broadcasts the international news. I am certain that my family and friends back in the United States are keeping an eye on the same coverage in hopes of understanding what I'm doing. They are all worried, but in my brief calls I have convinced them that everything will be fine.

The sights and sounds of the lobby invade my senses. Where before the lobby had been filled with the faces of somber families, it is now filled with enthusiastic arrivals that have come to celebrate the traditional holiday festival. They are oblivious to what our staff and families have gone through, unaware that just a few miles away, four airplane-crash survivors are in the hospital, happy to have the greatest gift of all: one more day.

I push past the crowds and move towards the ballroom where my family awaits. The celebration is in full swing and the tragedy at hand seems magnified against it. Just inside the ballroom rests a long table scattered with sections of the local newspaper. In the center page, which someone has opened and displayed, there are photos of at least thirty American lawyers advertising to the families. The text below the ads is printed in Spanish and English, and promise big rewards for calling. It is estimated that there are hundreds of lawyers here already. My family is huddled in the center of the ballroom, and I find them immediately. They are hunched forward, as if a large invisible hand presses them towards the ground. A little boy no more than five stands beside them.

"*Hola*, my name is Tammy." I bend at the knees and meet the boy at eye level, offering a smile. He glares at me angrily.

"Hello," the man says. He introduces his wife, who nods politely. "We are waiting for news."

I know what the news they are waiting for entails. It is news about their loved ones, and it will not be good. In their eyes I see sadness, concealed by an occasional forced smile and awkward glances. It is a sadness that will never go away.

"Yes," I say, acknowledging his statement. I try to smile yet not smile, and at the same time consider a solution. We could wait here, but there is nothing to do and the room is embarrassingly desolate. There are no plants, no food, and no tables except the one at the door.

"Are you interested in getting something to eat?" I ask. "I'll work on getting your luggage back so you can have a fresh change of clothes."

The man and woman exchange words in Spanish and it is several long moments before they answer. The boy stares, but does not utter a word.

"*Hola*," I offer.

The boy clings to his grandfather's leg, but in one swift movement jerks forward and spits at me.

"*Feo! Malo!*" he shouts, turning away. "*Feo!*"

"I'm sorry," the man says, pulling the boy close. "He only knows you are with the airline. He does not know you are not personally responsible."

"It's okay, I'm sorry...what is he saying?"

The silence that follows is awkward. We have planned for this in training, but I do not know an easy way to fill it.

"We could have coffee and some food," the grandfather says. "We have had nothing."

Crash victims and their families are acting on autopilot. They eat little, often nothing at all. The families of crash victims will respond with words they have never said in the past and will have conversations they will not remember in the future, conversations about death, about bringing home the remains of their loved ones. They will not be themselves physically, emotionally, or spiritually, because everything in their world has been shattered. I have prepared myself for the anger and I have prepared myself for sadness, but I have not prepared myself for the politeness my family offers me. I do not know the meaning of the little boy's words, but later, when I ask Hector about it, he tells me the words mean "bad" and "ugly." *Feo, malo.* The little boy had said the words with hatred in his eyes.

"Let's go find a quiet spot in the restaurant," I suggest.

It will be an impossible task, but it is the only option for food. We move through the lobby passing an attorney from Miami who has lingered there all day, but he does not dare to approach. The hotel security guards have been advised to keep a watchful eye. The reporters can stay and the attorneys can linger, but if a family member is approached on hotel property, the staff will ban them from the hotel. The security guards are unnecessary because there is no way any attorney will corral my family.

I run through the Emergency Response Team procedures in my head. Meeting a family for the first time is considered a critical task, and there are five common elements to consider. I have been taught that I must be factual, direct, compassionate, and focused. I must offer only the facts, nothing more. I must offer words of condolence and be genuine, not false. I must be specific, be careful not to promise what I cannot deliver, and I must always stay focused on the task at hand. I must keep myself healthy and sound, because the family I am assigned to will need a solid foundation during a time when theirs has been shaken. They will need a person who is consistent to handle their needs during an unpredictable time. I must eat sizable meals instead of candy bars, and get plenty of sleep. Taking care of myself will allow me to take care of them. The most important part of the interaction with a family is responding agreeably and determining their needs as expeditiously as possible.

I find my family a private table away from any other and pause before sitting, until they have chosen their preferred seats. The waitress brings menus and I wait while they read through them.

At a table across the restaurant there are four Emergency Response Team members drinking coffee and juice and talking quietly. Among them is Larry Duncan, the staff psychologist, who I have seen huddled in corners with team members throughout the day. He is well educated, in his mid-forties, and an inviting soul, quick to offer a smile. He is a valuable player in the activation process and beyond, because he and his team will be responsible for making sure the Emergency Response Team workers leave healthy and stay healthy. If it is a family member who requests a psychologist, Larry will drop everything for a quick, on-the-spot session. If I am experiencing stress myself or know of a team member who is coming apart, the same rule applies. The psychologists are versed in the effects of post-traumatic stress disorder and have counseled the victims and survivors of previous crashes. If a family member needs it, the airline will recommend full counseling services, but we are not to be counselors ourselves.

The waitress arrives with water and I am thankful for the interruption. She offers a warm smile, but when she talks to the little boy he does not respond. She does not know why he is here. Nearby, there are other children that splash and shout playfully in the pool.

We are separated by a clear plastic tarp, and it's a mistake I do not notice until it's too late. The silence among us is unbearable against the screams of the children. I stare out at the pool, silently willing them to stop, but they do not. When I look back at the table, the man and the woman and the little boy are staring, too, their faces blank and drawn.

A little girl splashes, and her long, wet hair and butterfly-print bathing suit remind me so much of last summer in the pool with my brother's child. I imagine how we would all feel if it had been my niece on that plane, and I *feel* the ache of losing her, and then more images assault me until I am overwhelmed. A knot forms in my throat and threatens to exit in a flood of tears, and for the first time, I feel empathy. All along I have felt sorry for them, but for the first time I feel that I am just a hair away from where they are. I think of my father and the pain the family went through after his shocking death, and it is too much. All at once, the images come, inconveniently triggered for some strange reason by the children in the pool. I have heard others say that there is a reason for everything, but I can find no reason for this.

"I'll follow up on your luggage and everything else," I blurt, rising from my chair. I push back from the table and the glass top teeters, sliding the salt and pepper shakers to the edge. I move away from the table and dash through the restaurant, inhaling deeply to keep in the emotion. As I run through the lobby, I see the others, and then Hector, who bounds towards me. I turn and follow the wall to the elevators, and luck is with me because one opens, drawing me inside. The doors close swiftly and there is a man, but the elevator rises and he exits on the next floor. I press the button for six, and then press two more buttons to confuse Hector or anyone else that has followed. I do not want to be seen, and on six I run from the elevator and race down the hall until the tears come, forcing me to stop. I hurtle forward and vomit in the base of a planter, in the cold dirt beneath the leaves of a potted plant. I gather myself together, take several deep breaths, and walk back to the elevator again.

Downstairs, I make several passes around the lobby until I am sure my eyes have dried. My head throbs, and my contacts feel like dried pebbles in my eyes. Beside the check-in desk, an Emergency Response Team staff member has set up an accounting office for the purpose of distributing funds to team members and families. I find the woman manning it and ask her how I can obtain two thousand dollars for my family, whose luggage we have lost.

"They'll need a rental car, clothes, incidentals. Their relatives have not been found, so they'll be here awhile."

"Have you filled out one of these?" The woman holds up a stack of forms.

"No. Not yet."

"Here. Fill them out and return them as soon as possible."

I take the forms and move to a different part of the lobby, where no one can see me. I complete all the information, including my name, title, the name of my family, and what the money is intended for. I return five minutes later with the completed documents, which the woman takes and places in a file folder. My heart sinks. I have no confidence that the forms will be looked at and that my family will get their money.

"Look," I say, "I feel terrible that on top of everything else, we lost their luggage. Is there anything we can do to speed things up?"

"Keep checking back with us. We'll let you know."

When I return to the table, the family is sitting like three stone statues. The boy has not moved and stares directly at the table. The man and woman do not smile.

"I'm hoping we'll have your funds soon," I tell them, trying to keep things positive. In truth, I'm enraged that I cannot just get the money right away. I have been told that we have thousands of dollars of cash on hand.

The wife folds her hands in her lap, fingering a beaded rosary.

The stones are dark, and she turns them in her fingers, running her thumb along the long strand of beads. I do not give much thought to the rosary or what it represents, only to the darkening silence between us. God was not there for the people of Flight 965, I think. At this point, I am unable to understand how this day will be branded on my soul for eternity.

"Excuse me," the man says. "Can you tell us anything more than what we know?"

It is the question I have feared, because I do not know any more than he does. The information has trickled in to the command center, and the recovery process has been slower than everyone would like.

I shake my head. "No, nothing more. I'm sorry."

The silence is deep. The man lowers his head and turns to his wife, translating what I have said. We sit and watch the activities of those around us without exchanging a word, and time seems to have stopped. I am outside of myself, and, though every table is occupied, the sounds are muted and my ears are hollow. It is the same sensation that one gets during the descent of an airplane, as if we are enclosed in a vacuum. It is as if someone has orchestrated this scene, and I am a character thrust into a dark cave with these strangers. After an hour passes, we are the same. Around us, tables turn over as the tourists who have arrived for the holiday come and go.

On the table between us, a laminated card displays a photograph of cheesecake and a description of other desserts. I push the card toward the boy, who is now curled into the nook in his grandfather's outstretched arm.

"Would you like some dessert?" I ask, expecting to make him smile.

Instead, the boy recoils and a scowl crinkles his forehead. It is a defiant expression, and he pushes his face into his grandfather's side so that I cannot look at him.

Across the restaurant, a man flails his arms, summoning me. I exhale deeply, grateful for the reprieve.

"Excuse me," I say. "I think someone has something for me. I'll be right back."

I walk quickly and the man pulls me to the side.

"You're Tammy, right? You've got the family from New Jersey? We lost their bags?"

"Yes."

"Well, good news. I've got their money and we may have their bags to them within twenty-four hours. I think they ended up on another airplane somehow." He hands me a plain white envelope containing the cash and asks me to sign a receipt.

"Thank you," I say, breathing an extended breath. It is one small victory in a day of none.

When I return to the table, I hand the money to the grandfather and offer to take them wherever they need to go.

"No," he says. "We will go. Thank you. We have relatives here that we can call."

The waitress brings the check and the family leaves me alone to pay it. I bid them good-bye and feel relieved when they turn the corner into the lobby.

# chapter sixteen

# Sifting for Clues

On an evening eleven days after the crash, we gather together as a team at several small tables in the apex of the lobby. Julie has decided to forfeit the dinner, preferring to remain in our hotel room. She said she would order dinner from room service, and after the first round of drinks, I wish I had done the same. It is an awkward crowd and I am socializing with strangers. We have a large company—at last count over one hundred thousand employees—and I have never met any of these people until now, except for the few I saw during the training class.

After the second round of drinks, George Jones commands the waitress to deliver the check. It has been a long day among a series of long days, but no one complains. Only five passengers had been pulled alive from the wreckage, and one succumbed to the injuries. Our complaints are insignificant compared to the enormity of it all.

Although the survivors are in serious condition, they are expected to resume normal lives. "Normal" being an entirely different definition, of course, for the survivor of an airplane crash, because there can probably be no normal again and no return to the way it was before the airplane dropped out of the sky.

We have all learned in training that although the survivors of the plane crash have escaped death, they are likely to suffer serious and prolonged psychological injuries on top of any physical injuries they may have. Post-traumatic stress disorder may be present and may manifest itself in dreams, actions, or through depression or addiction.

Every evening I have had vivid, colorful dreams about the people, the crash, and the survivors. One involved a middle-aged man peering out at me from an airplane window, screaming for help. I am desperate to rescue him, but he does not get out. I watch from a position above him, as if I am watching a movie. I feel as if I *am* him.

I have not heard anyone here complain about stress. I suspect it is because everyone works hard to appear strong. The woman I encountered in the airport, who was sent home, was an anomaly, and I have heard no one speak of her. Everyone else seems incredibly strong, and I am surprised by how strong I am myself. But what we all know deep inside is what we learned before we came, that the stress can kick in, and if it does, those afflicted with it are often unable to recall things they have seen. They subconsciously block the trauma from their mind and could live with it bottled up inside for years.

"Take your identification badge off," Jones barks at the young man sitting beside me. He is a twenty-five-year-old ticket agent from New Orleans and the name badge clipped to his pocket identifies him as Jonathan. He has attended training class like the rest of us and is aware of the strict code of conduct to which all team members are required to adhere. Among them is the rule that no identification badges are to be worn in public places, so that the press cannot easily spot airline employees. Another rule involves the consumption of alcohol while wearing any airline uniform or identification badge, a cardinal sin that can result in termination. Jonathan promptly removes the badge.

The ethical standards and qualities we must possess as members of the Emergency Response Team are clear. Among them is leadership, even though many of the employees have never been in leadership roles. For some, their daily duties as an airline employee entail loading bags into a plane, with minimal interaction with others. But we have been taught that leadership is not a position; leadership comes from within.

At our table the conversation is professional, but there are whispers from two women beside me about the possibility of sabotage on 965. There are lawyers and reporters all over the lobby, but the women don't seem to notice. I glare at the women, trying to warn them to stop, but they ignore me. Across the corridor, the attorney from Miami who has aggressively pursued our families pretends to read a magazine. He is dressed in a suit that looks like Armani and his hair is slicked back. He has worn expensive loafers every day with long pants and linen shirts. He tries to be inconspicuous by blending in with the crowds, but he is far too good-looking and memorable. We have been warned to stay away from him.

At the table to our left, a Hispanic man in a white suit barks orders to a waitress and three bottles of expensive champagne appear. His loudness commands our attention. A girl rises from her chair and perches herself on his lap as he pours one glass for her, then another for himself. She is stunningly beautiful and her thick hair falls just below her halter-top. But she is no more than fourteen and she is scantily clad in a silvery miniskirt that exposes miles of legs. She keeps her hand on his shoulder and stares at him with adoring eyes. I can't take my eyes off of them as I try to understand how it can be. In America, the man would be taken away and arrested for child molestation. Here, I am the only one who seems to care.

"The engines are being examined right now," Jonathan offers. He takes a long swig from the beer glass and glances at George, who is embroiled in an animated conversation with the others.

I nod and turn away, but it does not deter him.

"Looks like the airplane struck nose up," Jonathan whispers, "which means the pilots had obviously tried to pull out of it at the last minute. My source at the crash site says that the left engine had soil and branches and stuff in it, and the right engine was buried halfway in the ground."

"Let's talk about this another time."

Jonathan shrugs, rolling his eyes.

The investigation is being conducted by a Colombian group called the Aeronautica Civil of the Republic of Colombia, located in Bogota. Once the organization has completed its investigation, a full report would be issued.

After awhile, Mr. Jones suggests that we all take taxis to a nearby restaurant to enjoy a peaceful, private dinner away from the eyes of everyone else. We move to the curb, pile into several taxis, and proceed in a long line of cars. There are four people crammed into ours.

"You been to the crash site?" whispers Jonathan, settling into the backseat beside me.

"No, not yet."

"I can take you up there." His breath smells rancid, of peanuts and alcohol.

"No, I'm not sure I need to go up there unless I'm asked by the team."

"But I know how to get there and we can sneak up there tonight if you want."

I am curious about the crash site, but I have no intention of going anywhere with Jonathan, who seems like a loose cannon who will eventually self-destruct.

"Our people were shot at yesterday by some rebels in the area," he says. "They've blocked it off now and I doubt they'll be sending anyone else up. We had to get everyone out by helicopter, just like the bodies."

"Doesn't sound like we should be up there."

"I went up. The plane is everywhere, spread out in small pieces. I think it was a bomb."

I ignore the comment and wonder how he ever got here. The experts have almost completely ruled out a bomb, though certain media organizations keep putting out stories on that possibility.

"But there have also been rumors of pilot error," I say. "It could be that, could be anything."

"Hey, there are all kinds of rumors but someone could have easily snuck a bomb on board. Bombs these days are pretty high-tech.

You can put them into a radio and no one would even know. The best ones are made of plastic. RDX, in fact. Rapid detonation explosive. It's a plastic explosive capable of demolishing large objects within seconds. It's almost never detected by those airport sensors."

"You know way more about bombs than you should," I tell him.

"I researched all that stuff for a paper in college."

The taxi pulls to a stop in front of a small restaurant and our group stands just outside the door while George converses with the proprietor in halted Spanish. In minutes, the tables are rearranged and we are seated at a series of small square slabs pushed together to form one large table in the center of the room. There are thirteen of us, a mixture of seasoned and inexperienced Emergency Response Team members and some who have worked previous crashes. We settle into our chairs and look at the menus a waitress has handed out.

"Can you interpret this for me?" asks Ben, a flight attendant from Nashville. He pushes the menu towards me. His thin face is animated, marked by large dimples. He has an effeminate manner and gestures softly with his hands as he speaks.

"Sorry, I'm not much better at Spanish." I smile. "Just order whatever George orders, that might be the safest bet."

"Good thinking."

The food arrives on simple white plates, and I dig in immediately. The dish is a local concoction of chicken surrounded with yellow rice inside a palm leaf. The restaurant smells like an open-air market, a mixture of meat, teas, herbs, and various spices. I prod the meal with my fork and take a large bite. The chicken is soft and moist and goes down easily. I take several bites of the thinly sliced plantains that surround the plate, washing them down with water. The plantains are miniature versions of a banana, cooked in oil until they are slightly brown.

At the table beside us, a local man and woman eat what looks like the same thing. They speak animatedly amongst themselves, ignoring the foreigners who have just arrived. At our table the talk is mostly social, but some converse quietly about the crash. I have heard several different versions of the dog story, including that Milagro was found in a tree, and then another that he was found in the cargo hold, shivering. I have learned not to place much stock in the stories that come in, because even amongst our small, close-knit group, the rumors turn into elaborate tales that become more fantastical with each telling. We have been placed in a unique circumstance and the stories are told as the tellers remember them.

In training, we had been taught the importance of security. After a series of commercial aircraft hijackings in the seventies, security in the industry was increased and passengers were required to undergo a screening by a metal detector before entering the concourse leading to the departure gate. Shortly thereafter, airlines began the process of screening carry-on luggage, followed by an increase in security procedures surrounding the aircraft itself, in order to prevent sabotage or the placement of bombs on board. Security is tight within our company; airplanes are guarded throughout the night and parked in secured areas. Anyone who services the aircraft is subject to an inspection, and every cabin, cockpit, and cargo hold is inspected prior to the first flight of the day.

Although the larger airports around the world have grown into sophisticated security practices, here they are far behind. Latin America has the second worst safety record of any region, behind Africa, yet foreign carriers fly in because the money is here. Travelers and businesses will board a flight to Latin America, so airlines will offer the flight.

The one thing the scanners have had trouble detecting in the past are the vast amount of drugs that continue to enter the United States via internal body carriers, which are the human mules used to transport cocaine and other drugs through ingestion. Airlines face this problem despite the ongoing security and prevention mechanisms deployed by the Drug Enforcement Administration because mules have gotten through the airport system, sometimes carrying as much as one kilo of cocaine or heroin in their intestines. They do this through a dangerous process in which they fast for three or four days, ingest cooking oil for lubrication, and then swallow the drug packets encased in condoms.

Often the mules transporting the drugs are desperate, innocent victims of the drug trade. Some are just elderly people desperate to provide for their families. The packets are pushed down their throats with hands or pliers and positioned in their esophagus for travel. If the packet bursts, the individual dies. Often, the packet erodes from the acid in the stomach and the drugs seep into the internal organs like poison. This is a slow and painful death.

If the mule survives, however, he or she is taken to a hotel room by drug gangs on the other end and given laxatives until the drugs are expelled. It is a fate not much better, and no amount of security can prevent the transportation of illegal substances from third-world countries, because the individuals are so desperate to survive that the easy money is a constant temptation. The airplane is the fastest method of transporting humans, cargo, and substances, and for that reason it is always the first choice. Even with industry safeguards, preventing criminals, drugs, and other illegal matter from boarding planes is nearly impossible. At some point or another, something gets through.

Much of the talk at the table has been about the mountain, and most think that what's left of the airplane parts will be collected by a contracted aircraft salvage company and transported to America for examination. Once there, the fragments will be tested for chemical compounds as well as evidence of the physical indications of the cause of the crash, including markings resulting from an explosive device.

A woman from Boston wonders if any of us will suffer from post-traumatic stress disorder, launching us into a discussion about the multitude of emotions we may face. Recognizing the symptoms in ourselves and others would be an important part of the process. The things we see here, combined with our exposure to the grief of family members, could contribute to secondary traumatic stress. Studies had shown that in the past, government investigators who had responded to crisis activations were shown to have the effects of post-traumatic stress disorder as many as six to nine months following an airplane crash. Some of these workers had interviewed survivors and family members of the victims, while others had been exposed to the frantic voices of the pilots in their final minutes of flight after listening to the cockpit voice recorder.

I have wondered about the stress I'll feel after the crash, but I doubt that it will affect me. Soon the crash will be forgotten, overshadowed by the crashes that will inevitably follow. It is a cynical view, but a realistic one. The crash and the way it affects me is irrelevant. Others have faced much worse than I will face, and in the future, far worse tragedies will leave their imprint.

In the cab back to the hotel, Jonathan pushes himself into the backseat beside me. My window is halfway open, and the air outside seems magical, so fragrant and light that I cannot help but realize how empty the sky must have been in the final moments before the airplane went down. The sky that seems so appealing on this night was on that one unforgiving, a sky in which moments earlier a passenger may have enjoyed its glories from the view and safety of the airplane window.

He directs the driver to a local discothèque.

"I'm not going," I say when the car pulls to a stop. The girls who rode with us from the restaurant file out with him and head for a tiny door off the side street blaring with disco music.

"Come on!" Jonathan persists.

"I'm wiped," I say. "I'll head back to the hotel."

"Don't know what you're missing." He closes the door and the taxi pulls away.

# chapter seventeen

# The Buddy Program

In the hotel room, Julie has already claimed the bathtub. An opera drifts under the door and a room-service tray sits on the bed. I undress, find the terry cloth robe and slippers, and reach for a bar of chocolate from housekeeping.

"Have a good day?" she asks. Her voice is muffled behind the door.

"Depends on what you mean by that. Is it possible to have a good day down here?"

"I suppose not," she says.

"I was assigned to a family."

In moments, Julie emerges from the bathroom wrapped in a towel. Her hair is not wet, but the rest of her is, and the drops of water bead in a trail down her lanky legs. She reaches for a bottle of water and sits on the edge of the opposite bed.

"You're kidding," she says.

"Nope. A mother and father, and their grandson."

"So what did you think…how did you take it?"

I remove several pages of notes from my briefcase and begin to shred them by hand. I tear the conversations and personal notes I have made regarding my assigned family into tiny squares, then tear the tiny squares once more before dropping half into one wastebasket and half into my suitcase. If half are in my suitcase, I reason, no one will be able to retrieve them from the garbage or make sense of anything written on the half they have found.

"Fine," I reply. "I don't think it'll be a problem."

"Yeah right...I had a family myself once, so I know you're lying."

"When were you assigned to a family?"

"In the last activation I worked."

Julie has appeared cool and disconnected, and I imagine the assignment has not affected her. I envision her working with a family and answering their questions in a professional manner. I am embarrassed that I could not keep it together. Gratefully, no one had seen me. I can see why they have assigned her as my buddy. The program has been designed to place a weak link in the chain with a stronger one, and she is clearly the strongest link. She is someone I can learn from and I want to soak it in like a sponge.

"I won't do it again," she admits. "This time I told them no way."

"Really, why?"

"It was just too hard...I keep in touch with him still."

The last sentence is a confession, because to continue to see or correspond with a family member of a crash victim is forbidden, an action punishable by termination from the company.

"Don't repeat that," she says suddenly. "I haven't told anyone. I'll deny it if you do and so will he. He loves me."

"Who is *he*?"

"His name is Charlie. I was assigned to him after his wife died in our last crash. I had to spend a lot of time with him. He needed a lot of attention and comforting, and then I attended the funeral...you can't imagine...." Her voice trailed off.

"Yes, I think I can."

"I'll never forget the look on his face when I told him that his wife's body had been positively identified."

"How old is he?"

"He was eighty-two at the time of the plane crash. We just celebrated his eighty-sixth birthday. But it all started with one lunch.

Charlie called me about a month after the funeral. He was so alone, had no children, and didn't really know what to do with himself. He couldn't drive and, since I had taken him everywhere for about a month during the crash activation, I guess he thought it was still okay to call me and ask me to take him to the grocery store. I couldn't say no. So then we had lunch. It was on a Wednesday and it turned into lunch every Wednesday. Then it turned out to be a situation where I was getting more from him than he was getting from me. He spends every Christmas with me and my family now."

"I can understand that."

I smile. She is far more than the corporate soldier I had pegged her to be, and she has followed her heart despite rules that strictly forbade her to. I wonder how many others have maintained friendships with the people to whom they had been assigned.

"It was beyond my control, really. I know it's against the rules but I'll be out of here soon anyway. I almost didn't come to this activation but I felt like I had to, because if I said no it could have hurt my chances for promotion."

She moves to the closet and pulls out a pair of pajamas with long cotton pants and a long-sleeved shirt. A moment later she emerges from the bathroom fully dressed and climbs into bed.

"You know there's a reward out for one of the bodies," she says.

"I had heard that but didn't know if it was true."

"It is. One of the passengers who hasn't been found yet. A boy supposedly connected with the drug cartel. His family has a reward out for his body. Word is that someone stole it."

"Who?" I ask.

"Some local looking for money."

"You're kidding…I mean, where are they going to hide a body?"

"Anywhere," she says. "House, farm, backyard. Somewhere close to the crash site. It'll be all over the papers, I'm sure."

Diffusing publicity is something that we and every other airline are used to. The newspapers are always reporting the details of litigation, whether it is a passenger who sues because of injuries sustained during turbulence, flight attendants who sue because of secondhand smoke, or some other issue.

Before this crash, someone had threatened a lawsuit over the use of the profile passenger system, a common practice among airlines to safeguard the skies. Ticket agents were trained to identify a profile passenger by certain characteristics, such as a male passenger of Middle-Eastern descent who travels alone, pays with cash, and has a one-way ticket only. All of these ingredients could add up to a profile of someone who could be a suspected terrorist and a threat to the airline's security. Yet not every person who fits this specific profile would be a threat, and some individuals capitalized on this profiling to create unnecessary publicity and controversy for the airline. All along, it was the airline's intention to keep the passengers safe by identifying certain high-risk passengers who had been a previous threat to our nation's air carriers.

"You're going to have to perform an ante mortem for your family," Julie says.

"Why do you say that?"

"Because there are a lot of bodies that haven't been identified. Have you studied up on it?"

"They taught us about it in training. It's the process of setting up a meeting with the family member and asking all those horrible questions."

"Right."

"I rode in from the airport with an ERT member who had to perform one. A sales manager from Boston named Barbara. I saw her yesterday at the command center. She performed an ante mortem on a child."

I turn out the light and we talk for another hour. Julie falls asleep, but I cannot stop thinking about the ante mortem. Everyone who has done one has described it as a difficult assignment, mainly because of the intrusive questions that must be asked.

\*   \*   \*

Earlier in the day, I had crossed paths with Barbara again at the command center, and we had talked for half an hour. The ante mortem she performed was for a ten-year-old girl. Because Barbara was fluent in Spanish, she was chosen for the task.

*Head downstairs to the lobby,* the Emergency Response Team staff member had instructed. *The parents are waiting for you.*

Barbara took the elevator down, file in hand, and walked into the lobby, scanning name badges for the family members to whom she had been assigned. The mother of the child was about her age, and dressed in an expensive taupe pantsuit. Her husband wore a collared, button-down shirt, and everything seemed in place. Unlike the other families in the lobby, their clothes were neat and pressed. They did not seem disheveled and their arms were locked together.

"Have you found our daughter?" asked the man. It was the first thing out of his mouth when he saw Barbara walk up.

"No, I'm sorry, Mr. Osterman. Not yet." She had been direct and forthcoming. She could not let them have false hope. "Can we go somewhere quiet and sit down? I have a few questions I need to ask you."

Mr. Osterman was an attorney. Mrs. Osterman had been in the banking industry for many years. Both were adept at managing through a crisis and were handling this one in a professional manner. There was work to do to find their daughter, they reasoned, and if they cooperated, perhaps they would find out that she had survived. They would not lose hope.

"What color are Elizabeth's eyes?" Barbara asked.

"Blue," her father answered.

"Are there any distinguishing marks on her body, such as a scar, that we should be aware of?"

"She has a birthmark the size of a quarter on her thigh," said the mother.

Barbara asked question after question, and the answers came without hesitation. It had gone too well, but she was afraid that the tattoo question, as ridiculous as it would seem, would cause them to explode. But the question had to be asked.

"Did Elizabeth have any tattoos or body piercings?" Barbara asked. "I know she was young…"

"We had her ears pierced when she was a baby, replied the mother. She wore pink stud earrings on the plane. Like diamonds, only a pink stone, not real."

When Barbara finished with the ante mortem she immediately went to her room and mixed herself a rum and Coke, using the miniature bottles of rum she had taken from a previous flight. She drank three and went back to her work. The following day, the little girl was found and identified. She was not found alive.

*  *  *

I am several days into the crisis but I have read only 10 percent of the crisis manual, mainly because the possibility of a crash seemed so far away before. Not only will I need to comprehend what I am doing and saying and communicating to the victim's families, but I will need to understand what's going on all around me, on the ground, at the crash site, and at the morgue. If a family member has a question, I will need to know the answer.

I move to the bathroom and close the door, spreading the manual out onto the tile in front of me. I read everything about the process of emergency response, beginning with the first tab. There are many things I've learned about plane crashes in my career with the airline, because I have read newspaper articles on my industry and done research over the years to stay informed on industry events. I know, for instance, that when an airplane goes down, the disaster zone it creates can immobilize a community's emergency system. The Emergency Response Team is affected directly, but the community is affected indirectly. In the United States, every airport has specific procedures in place to deal with crashes on site, but the community outside the airport gate usually does not, especially in a small city. In poor countries such as this one, the communities are already plagued by poverty, and any further destruction to houses, villages, or farmland can be economically devastating.

If a city is not versed in disaster relief, the result is confusion and a lack of knowledge about how to handle an immediate, major disaster. Local firefighters who have never experienced a plane crash before will be subjected to the dismembered remains found at a crash site, something they may not have ever prepared themselves for. A forensics lab will be established and refrigerated trucks driven in to keep the bodies from decomposing, and hundreds of investigators will converge on the scene in order to begin the process of identifying the dead. The latest in technology will be used in this process along with specialized investigative tools used in morgues with which local rescue personnel may not be familiar.

In an airplane rescue operation, confusion can exist on many levels because there are at least three governing bodies involved at all times: the Federal Aviation Association, the National Transportation Safety Board, and the local governing officials, in addition to the local, national, and international rescue teams. Most communities have emergency action plans, but few have specific air-disaster plans that contain the precautionary steps emergency and city personnel would take in case one occurred. Here in Cali, the community is poor and ill-equipped to handle a disaster of this magnitude. No one could have prepared for something like this.

*   *   *

It is late into the night, but sleep still eludes me. I am wired with adrenaline and anxious to see what the next few days will hold. I move back into the bedroom and slide into bed, but I stare at the ceiling in the darkness. Small noises come from the other sound of the room, where Julie is involved in a dream. She whimpers, says something unintelligible, then whimpers again until I wonder if I should wake her up. Julie has been through all of this before, but it seems to me that she has had enough. On the outside she is hard, able to talk about the activation with ease. Yet her eyes had filled up when she spoke of Charlie, and it seems that her feelings about being on the team have changed. After a minute, the whimpering from the next bed stops and there is silence. I move back to the bathroom and open the manual again.

# chapter eighteen

# Life

When I open my eyes in the morning, the first thing I see is the page on Colombia from the Emergency Response Team manual scattered across the cold bathroom floor. My face is pressed into the binder on the bathroom tile, where I had fallen asleep and slept soundly for hours.

I imagine the time to be four or five in the morning, judging from the depth of darkness outside the bathroom window, yet there is no confusion upon waking, like there was during nights at home when I would stumble from a dream into reality, confused about where I was. The dreams had been exactly the same since childhood, waking me with sobs, leaving me with a darkness that stayed with me all day. Dreams of a search for my father, traveling on a train in the dark of night, getting off at a desolate stop where there were no other people or sign of life. Being lost, in a foreign place, in the dead of night. Something I had yet to figure out was that the nightmare never followed me when I traveled, as if the Devil could not find me when I was sleeping in a hotel room.

* * *

At the command center it's noon and there is a lull in the activity, allowing Larry Duncan, team psychologist, an opportunity to meet with us. Larry will facilitate a mandatory psychological debriefing for all Emergency Response Team members followed by an update from

George Jones. Across the room, John North sits at the same spot at his table. We have all been told to be here now, but John has been here every morning, every afternoon, and every night. When the staff invited him for dinner, he refused. He has not slept as far as I can tell, and I imagine that his hotel room has been empty, just a storage place for his luggage. I have attempted to make small talk with him, but he is impossible to reach. In the evenings, he goes off on his own to the balcony for a smoke, or away for a beer. He returns red-faced and disheveled, on the edge of a precipice all by himself.

I recline in a chair and immerse myself in the newspaper some-one has brought in from the United States. A blurb on the sports page reminds me that a few years ago at this time, I was reading on the bal-cony of a resort in Florida, at a celebrity golf tournament hosted by our airline. I had spent the day driving Joe Namath and Dan Marino around in a cart and making sure our corporate clients were where they needed to be. That's the glamorous part of the job, I think.

First Officer Don Williams has a magnetic smile that haunts me from the front page of the international news section. At thirty-nine, he would have had a long future of flying ahead of him, a future sur-rounded by the love of three small children and a wife. The article contains profiles of several of the passengers, along with pictures of the smiling men and women.

In the photograph, the first officer displays a broad smile, the kind of smile that envelops the heart of a stranger having the worst of days. He seems like the kind of guy who would go out of his way to hand out airplane wings, the kind of guy who would go back to the cabin to search for children to bring to the cockpit.

The day before the accident, Williams had an appointment with an aviation medical examiner for a routine flight physical, which later resulted in an excellent health report. After the physical, he had lunch with his brother, played basketball with his children, and attended his son's basketball game with his wife after a family dinner. When they returned home, he helped put the children to bed. He had been a hands-on dad, a man who took care of himself and his family. He had been described by his colleagues as professionally competent and assertive and seemed to have a well-balanced life. On the day of the accident, he rose early in the morning to join his family for breakfast and help his wife prepare for their children's home-schooling activities. Later in the day, he worked out, then visited with his father and other family members. At 12:30, he left for the airport.

Captain Nick Tafuri was also an experienced pilot, but began his flying career much earlier than First Officer Williams. In the Air Force, Tafuri had flown a variety of military airplanes in domestic and foreign operations, acquiring thousands of flight miles. The captain had made several trips to this city in the past and knew it well. He was a non-smoker in excellent health and an avid tennis player with a wife and two children. The captain was known by colleagues for his strong communication skills and had received numerous letters from passengers and company employees that reflected outstanding performance. In the days leading up to the accident, the captain spent time relaxing, playing tennis with his wife, and visiting family in New Jersey. On the day of the accident, his wife prepared for her own trip as a flight attendant with the same airline.

The pilot had communicated with an airport control tower that operated twenty-four hours a day, controlling the traffic into and out of the city. Tafuri and Williams had prepared for landing on the nine thousand–foot runway. Everything should have gone smoothly. There had been no technical problems that should have prevented a safe landing, yet the airplane struck the ridge, crumbling into pieces. Investigators have found that the plane initially struck trees on the east side of the ridge, but that the majority of the wreckage had come to rest on the west side of the ridge.

The trail of impact was marked with broken and flattened trees, followed by a path of trees that had been completely uprooted. Along the beginning of the path, investigators found a trail of parts, including a fan cowling, the thrust reverser, and an engine fire bottle. The airplane struck the trees with its nose up, and the bulk of the wreckage came to rest at the top of the mountain. Investigators on site examined the engine and found the standard post-crash ingestion of soil, trees, and foliage, along with bent fan blades. The right engine was buried into the ground, but neither engine showed any pre- or post-crash indication of fire damage.

A rumor suspected to be a leak from an investigator has stated that the pilots might have made a wrong turn, which would mean that pilot error would be found as the cause of crash. It was not yet confirmed, but a Latin American aviation official has stated openly that the pilots had been off course.

*　*　*

Both pilots were experts and had adhered to the rigorous requirements set by the FAA. The Federal Aviation Administration requires commercial airline pilots to be at least eighteen, be fluent in English, and undergo instruction from an authorized instructor who has given the pilot specific, required ground training and certified that the individual is prepared for the required knowledge test applicable to the aircraft category sought. In addition, an individual applying for a commercial license must pass a series of aeronautical tests and must have a minimum number of flight hours.

The pilot of an aircraft has an immense responsibility that gives him control of hundreds of passengers' lives and a machine worth millions. The pilot is crowned the king of his aircraft, and during flight it's the pilot that calls the shots. He or she has the ability to determine if the airplanes are airworthy and the power to prevent unruly passengers from boarding. The pilot's best interests are protected by their unions, who work to ensure that they receive fair treatment for performing one of the most difficult jobs in the world.

Pilots must fight fatigue, stress, and performance challenges in the cockpit, and must maintain excellent health and vision to perform their jobs correctly. The FAA has established specific guide-lines for crew rest and flight-time regulations to decrease the effects of long hours in-flight. The takeoff and landing portion of flight is the most strenuous for a pilot, requiring an alert mind and quick reflexes. Everything in the middle is a series of monotonous activities designed to monitor flight equipment and controls. During a long flight, boredom can set in, and pilots must guard against it.

A multitude of factors can contribute to an accident, and the human element is just one. Aircraft aging and the way in which an airline maintains their aircraft is as important as the way the pilot maintains the craft in-flight. The airplane is a combination of a complex series of mechanisms and parts, and when one of them goes bad, disaster can occur. Seams can split, electrical systems can fail, and weather and numerous takeoffs and landings can wear the body. Determining the cause of an airplane crash occurs only after an exhaustive, multifaceted investigation based on all of the factors of flight combined.

*  *  *

"You okay?"

The voice startles me. I slam the newspaper on the table.

"You seem a bit lost in thought," Larry says, taking the chair beside me. "Have you had a debriefing since you've been here?"

"No, I'm fine."

"I'm available anytime, you know."

"No, really, I'm doing great. I was just reading about the pilots. The first officer was pretty young."

"About my age," he says. "So I heard you were assigned a family. How did it go?"

"Pretty well, I think. It's just frustrating trying to get them money. We lost their luggage, you know. After all they've been through and we can't even get their luggage here with them."

I do not tell Larry how I returned to the table by the pool and sat with the family for two more hours, unable to say anything compassionate or meaningful through my own frustration. I do not explain how frustrating it felt because I am afraid I'll wonder again if I had done enough, and that the memory of being with the little boy will cause my eyes to tear up. *We lost their luggage,* I had explained to a woman at the command center. *This family needs clothing, a new pair of underwear, some food. We need to get them their money.* I do not tell Larry how I completed the forms required to request the funds and how strange and tense it felt to be with the family as the time passed. There was nothing for the family to do but sit and wait in silence, something that I had never been good at.

"How did you handle working with the family?" Larry asked.

"I suppose as best as I could. They're going to buy some new clothes now. When we find their bag I'll make sure it gets to them." I will not tell him that it was too much for me, nor that it was at that moment that I realized just how hard this assignment could be. If he knows, there is the possibility that he would recommend I be sent home, like the woman I met in the airport on my way down. I will not take that chance.

Larry nods and smiles. "Well, just remember I'm here for you."

"Thanks, Larry."

I watch him walk away. The newspaper on the table is unfolded, exposing a photograph of one of the four survivors, the girl from Missouri. She smiles happily, and it seems like a photograph a reporter has dug up from a high-school prom or yearbook. Her lips are full and curved, revealing a flawless row of teeth, and her eyes are serious and dark. The structure of her face is strong. Mercedes Ramirez has robust cheekbones and magnificent dark hair, which is long and thick with envious curls. But she has lost her parents, and I expect that the long trip home will be the loneliest she has ever made. She will return to her sister, the one family member she has left.

On the mountain, search and rescue crews found her clinging to life. Although the plane had gone down in the evening, the wreckage was not found until early the next morning. Mercedes was found hours after that, after a full night in the jungle beside more than a hundred people who were killed upon impact, or in the process of dying. Search teams had arrived by helicopter to the crash site within a few minutes of seeing it from the air, but it had been more than twelve hours since the airplane went down, and just four passengers survived the wait. Investigators had originally determined that the magnitude of the impact and destruction of the airplane meant that no one could survive.

I tear the survivor's photograph from the paper and tuck it inside my wallet. She is almost my age, and she is a reminder that despite the valleys on the road ahead, all things are worth surviving. Maybe I'll find her someday and see how her life has turned out. My mind wanders into a daydream, and I wonder how my own life would turn out if the same thing happened to me, next year or the year after. Would I have the strength to go on?

# chapter nineteen

# Adjusting to the Real World

In the command center, the activity has died down and some of the employees sitting at the table make small talk about New Year's Eve and what they will do when they return home. I sit at the table and half-listen, making list after list of the tasks I know I'll have to complete here to finish up the activation, and then lists of what I'll do when I get home. The notebook I brought with me contains pages of lists, something I think I've begun doing in an effort to retain some sense of control. I make a list that will help me create my expense report when I get home from Cali, I make a list of groceries I'll need to buy, and another list of the projects I'll work on during the mandatory two weeks I'll have off from work.

My thoughts drift to the strangest of things, including New Years past, and how one year we can so strongly believe in one thing, but then the next year it is gone. I think of my brother, who seems so impervious to emotion, except for the smallest clues that give you a glimpse of what's really inside of him. On the wall in his bathroom in Dallas is a poem he had written as a child about his idol, Roberto Clemente, a baseball player who died in an airplane crash. Clemente had been the youngest of four children, raised in a barrio in Puerto Rico. He excelled in athletics and left his hometown to embark upon his dream of becoming a baseball player in the United

States, where he exceeded his goals and became the first Hispanic baseball player inducted into the Hall of Fame. During his remarkable career, Clemente led the Pittsburgh Pirates to two World Series titles, achieving a hit in every game. The little boy from the barrio became a twelve-time All Star, and the second baseball player to appear on a postage stamp, behind Jackie Robinson. But Clemente also had a strong desire to help others, a trait my brother admired most. On New Year's Eve in 1972, Roberto Clemente boarded a cargo plane in bad weather to take food, clothing, and medical supplies to earthquake victims in Nicaragua. His wife and friends begged him not to go, but he was worried that the victims were suffering, so he continued on with the trip. His airplane went down off the coast of Puerto Rico, and his body was never found. Investigators sifted for clues for days, but nothing linking them to Roberto's body emerged.

*  *  *

A staff member enters the room and announces that all but one of the bodies has been recovered.

"We just got word from the ground. Looks like we'll all be going home soon."

The room explodes. It has been twelve emotionally draining days since the airplane crashed into the mountain, and we are all far different now than when we first arrived.

The man takes a deep breath and waits for the applause to die down.

"But there's still one person missing," he cautioned. "So let's not get too excited until this thing is all wrapped up. Questions?"

There are none.

The psychologist has explained the four major dynamics we will all face upon returning home. The first is the reception we get from family members, which could range from extreme happiness to anger that we were away. The reaction from spouses, kids, and other members of the family may be different than we expect. We view ourselves as airline crisis-team members working to help others, he explains, but our family members may view us as selfish individuals who put others before our families. All of these things are important to understand and consider upon our return home. For those returning to an empty house, the lack of support from friends or loved ones can lead to severe depression. Getting connected with a network of friends for support will be key.

I have never before experienced an incident like this, and though I was not actually *on* the plane, the stories and encounters I've had have made me understand what it was like. I understand now everything they have told us in training, about how airplane-crash crisis workers may find the trivial concerns of the rest of the world difficult to understand. The worries and daily frustrations of family and friends will seem insignificant compared to the trauma we have seen and heard. Each day at the command center, the stories come in. John North is open about the details from the morgue, and the facts are inescapable. *The young man at the crash site, fighting off the investigators, crying because he wants to find his family. The father who flew to the crash site and spent the night in the jungle.*

Readjusting to the real world and a normal existence after days filled with trauma-based activities is likely to be daunting because we have seen and heard things that no one could imagine unless they have been through the same experience. My husband would not choose to be here and would decline it even if he were. My brothers think I'm crazy, my parents fear for my life, and my coworkers could care less. They have explained to us that our family members and coworkers may not even be interested in what we have seen, because they have other things going on in their lives. As important as this incident has been to the Emergency Response Team member, an outsider may not be able to empathize. I think about the flipside of what Larry has told us. I envision going home to a husband with a million questions I will not feel like answering. Questions about things I will not want to relive.

When I arrive home, I'll be packing my things, filing for divorce, and allowing both of us to move on. Life is too short, and if I didn't know it before, I know it now. I reread the questions on the worksheet and answer them in my head. What have I learned about life? What have I learned about others? What have I learned that can help me grow? I have learned not to take anything for granted. Today could be the last day I have.

# chapter twenty

# Concluding Contact

Our lives begin with fragments, single shards of memory from child-hood that mark the moment it all began. Ask someone to describe their first memory and they'll recall a four-year-old standing at the top of a driveway with a new toy. Ask someone else and they'll remember a nine-year-old and a completely different moment. Delve deeper, and you'll find that this one fragment of memory holds a feeling within it, an emotion that remains at the basis of our lives.

My own memory involves being alone in a small dark bedroom, shades drawn. There is no light or sound. I have been sent there to contemplate my behavior. I pick up the doll in the corner, the one with the large, cherubic face and rose-colored cheeks. I hoist her by her polka-dot dress and fling her into the air, landing my fist square against her jaw. The moment my tiny knuckles connect with plastic, her face caves in and she is ruined. I am not sorry, but filled with rage. I am no more than five.

When I think of the angry little boy from the family I was assigned to, I wonder if his very first memory will be this fragment; the rage he had felt at this terrible moment in time that cannot be easily for-gotten. Will the story of his life begin here?

New Year's Eve is approaching fast, and at home everyone is preparing for an evening of celebration along with the long day of football that follows. In the command center, I go to the assignment table and search for my name on the sheet of paper they've put out for the day. There will be no need for an ante mortem on my family, because the bodies of their son and daughter-in-law have been found and positively identified. I am half glad and half sad—glad because I won't have to ask them a hundred invasive questions and sad that their worst fears have been confirmed. Even when you know it already, how do you prepare to hear that your child is dead? I do my research and talk with several people until I discover that my family's luggage has been located. I feel a strange sense of accomplishment, like a starving child who happily receives a crust of bread for dinner. We have finally found their luggage, we have found their loved ones, and it's time to go home.

I flip through the manual and find the page on concluding contact. Concluding contact with a family would have to begin in small, methodical steps, not just one good-bye. One of the primary reasons for concluding all contact with a family is to help facilitate the family's healing so they can break off from external support and mend on their own. I wonder if they really feel that we've given them support, and I wonder if I would if the situation were reversed. Another important reason to conclude contact is to avoid the victim identification syndrome that often comes with exposure to someone else's grief. Grief is contagious and can spread like a cancer.

If a family member mentions anything about retaining a lawyer, we are to conclude contact immediately, with no further conversation. This would occur with one simple statement, which has already been prepared for us. Once contact has ended, any further interaction with the family will occur between the family and our corporate insurance department, which will handle any reimbursement claims or litigation. The insurance group within the airline is an integral part of the crisis aftermath and can arrange for immediate cash payments for items such as the morgue facility, supplies, or anything needed as a result of the crash. The personnel department at airline headquarters communicates closely with the insurance department to provide them with the employee numbers and emergency-contact information of any crewmembers that had been on board. Personnel will also forward any worker's compensation and insurance information, if applicable. All of these departments work together to make sure that the crash-recovery and reimbursement process is cohesive.

We have been advised to refrain from discussing any aspect of the crash investigation, even though we have been exposed to frequent updates about the cause from staff members during our time here. It is understood that the preliminary report from the Colombians is that the pilots had traveled off course, which led to the crash. There was no indication of any parts that fell off in the air. When investigators at the crash site analyzed the engines, they found that there was no evidence of fire damage and the fan blades were bent, damages that were consistent with standard impact. The damage to both engines was similar, except that the right engine was found slightly buried into the ground. Numerous parts were retrieved from the site, and anything deemed important, such as circuit cards with flight or navigational data, would be packed in a static-free material for shipment to the United States. At the laboratories of their manufacturers, the cards would be cleaned and analyzed, and the data reported back to the investigative team for inclusion in the final report.

Before departing Miami for Cali, the airplane had been in Guayaquil, Ecuador, and the Guayaquil to Miami flightcrew reported that there had been no maintenance or operations-related discrepancies. Captain Nick Tafuri and First Officer Donnie Williams had arrived at the Miami operations office one hour before the proposed departure time of 16:40, as is standard procedure. Although most of this is public knowledge by now, we are not to engage in speculation or discussion of any of it.

When we conclude contact with our assigned family, we are to expect questions and possibly even theories on the cause of crash.

We have been told to be prepared for anything and not to be alarmed or show surprise if no hand is offered when we reach out to shake theirs. The best response we can offer is to smile and nod, remaining aware of body language at all times.

\* \* \*

When it is time to conclude contact with my family, I think of anything else I might need, review their file, and head for the lobby. I step out of the elevator and the little boy is right there in front of me, standing with the same penetrating gaze as before. I take a deep breath and try to remember what the instructor had taught us about this moment. *Speak at a normal pace and attempt to control the pitch and tone of your voice. Don't become emotionally involved.*

It is all in the best interests of the families and makes practical sense. The last part truly helps me, because I realize immediately that the presence of the little boy is what throws me off, sending my emotions spiraling. I inhale and pause for several seconds to let them speak if they need to. *Listen,* I remind myself. *Listen, evaluate, respond.*

"Good afternoon," I say. "Is there anything else I can do for you right now, before you prepare for your flight home?"

The old man shakes his head, and the woman does, too. There is nothing more I can do for them.

I look at the little boy for only a second before returning to the adults. I do not want to think about his pain. I just want to be good at what I do and help them with whatever they need without getting involved in their life. I will not be like Julie and end up sharing Christmas dinner with someone I have been connected to by tragedy. I will perform my job as a professional and move on.

"Well then…" I say, fumbling for words. "I suppose it's time to say good-bye. I'll be heading back to the United States soon myself, but I want you to know that if you need anything at all, we'll be available." I hand them my business card, which has the telephone number of an Emergency Response Team staff member who will take any future calls from the family members.

"Thank you," the man says. He places the card in his pocket and offers his outstretched hand.

"You're welcome."

The woman forces a smile and I watch them as they turn and walk away.

# chapter twenty-one

# Saying Good-bye

In the morning it is still dark when Julie and I check out of the hotel. We pay the bill with our individual credit cards and keep the receipts to expense later. My half is over a thousand dollars and includes food from the mini-bar and the room charges.

There are no formal good-byes, only a quick hug from Julie.

"You can keep that," she says, referring to the navy-blue suit jacket I had borrowed and have worn all week.

"Are you sure? I guess I just put it on this morning out of habit."

"No, keep it," she says. "I insist. I won't be needing it."

"At least let me give you your company pin back…"

"No. I won't be needing that either."

The bellman gives a shrill whistle, summoning a taxi from the street. He packs my suitcase into the trunk with the others and frowns, bowing to kiss the top of my hand. He has summoned taxis for us every morning and night, and we have become fast friends. He is aware of why we have come here and has been a supportive and friendly face. Julie and I step into the cab along with one other woman from the team whom we have seen around the command center but have not worked with. We pack tight into the backseat and I am wedged between them, their breath and limbs against me with every turn. For the first time since I've been here, I cannot wait to get out.

I am used to the machine guns on every corner now, but I duck
instinctively when a soldier across the street raises the nose of his
rifle. It moves skyward and is flung behind him in one fast gesture
with the strap attaching it to his shoulder. The soldier wears fatigues,
as they all do, the deep, dark green like the soldiers in the United
States wear, with the tall, black, lace-up boots.

At the airport we check in, then go to a lounge that consists of a
sparse holding area littered with cigarettes. At the gate, a flight attendant takes our tickets, gives us boarding passes, and tells us to wait.
Flight attendants from the United States sit with their bags, and
when I am off this plane and home in bed, they will be in some other
airport waiting with their bags again. It is a job I cannot comprehend.
Each day and night boarding a plane for destination unknown. It's a
job that seems to have increasingly inherent risk. Each day that they
report for work could be their last.

When we arrive in Dallas, we'll be greeted by airline officials and
escorted to a special room in the terminal where a psychologist from
employee relations will be waiting to conduct a debriefing. Once
we're released, we will have a mandatory two weeks to do nothing
but reflect on where we've been and what we have seen. I have not
decided what I will do during my two weeks, but I know it will mean
seeing friends and loved ones and telling everyone how much I love
them.

On the plane ride home, the inside of the aircraft is eerily quiet.
I am seated in coach because of the nature of my trip. If there are
passengers on board who are family members of the victims and they
are seated in coach, I will want to be in coach, too. An airline that
puts the employees in first class and the victims in back could create
a field day for the media. Our first-class passengers will be served
caviar by doting flight attendants and will watch movies from the
comfort of warm leather seats.

I settle back into the stiff seat in coach and notice sitting a few
rows in front of me the parents of a flight attendant who had been on

the flight that crashed. The pages of my journal are filling fast with the experiences and emotions of the people around me. Each day I have taken great care to make notes of my surroundings, because it is the only way to process what I've seen and heard. My heart stills and the euphoria I felt in returning has disappeared I cannot help but watch them, huddled together. The clouds move swiftly outside the airplane window as our craft climbs the invisible stairway of flight. I hold my breath, as I never would have done before, and grip the seat. The sensation of gravity pushes me back as the plane thrusts forward, and for a moment the churning engines seem as if they just can't make it. But in seconds we level off and we are a soaring little radar dot among thousands in the sky.

Before the event, I had no fear of flying and flew with abandon. Trips to Paris for dinner at the restaurant on the upper level of the Eiffel Tower, then back again. A trip to New York to Christmas shop only to return on the very same day. A seven-day journey to Singapore to attend a dinner party with Sherpas, or a trip to the Swiss Alps for a four-day ski vacation. In my young life with the airline, I have been educated by travel, discovering new places and people along the way. I have not missed an opportunity to jump on a plane, regardless of where it was headed.

But now it will be different. I have presented the message of our airline's safety record over and over again to the corporations that I've been selling the airline to, and the logic remains at the forefront of my mind. Statistically, there are far fewer fatalities from air disasters each year than from traditional disasters such as automobile accidents and I have the PowerPoint presentations to prove it. The graphs and charts substantiate it all. Travelers today are so comfortable flying that the majority of the population has experienced air travel by the age of twenty-one.

For millions of business travelers, boarding an airplane is just another method of getting from one meeting to another. Better than a car, more practical than a boat. Travel is a constant in our lives. We plan weekends in the Hamptons, ski trips to Colorado, and weeklong jaunts to the Caribbean. We surf the Internet for the lowest fares to take our children on spring-break vacations, we sign up for airline Internet specials that will deliver us inexpensively to our families in other states. I know all of this, and I know that the airplane I am on has transported thousands of passengers before me over millions of miles. But when my hands grip the seat and my heart begins to race, I know that I have changed.

There is a long line for the bathroom in the back of the plane, so I use the one in first class. On the way back to my seat, I see Jonathan sitting in first class, drinking some form of alcohol in a tiny bottle. In the window seat beside him, an oblivious business traveler reads the paper.

"Hi Jonathan," I say, kneeling beside him. I lower my voice to a whisper. "Would you mind relocating? There are a few seats back behind me."

"What? No way! You're crazy. There's no problem with where I'm sitting. I'm staying here."

"Fine." I drop the issue and move back to my seat, knowing that the disturbance would be worse than the situation at hand. Everyone involved in this tragedy has already been through so much, especially the families.

The arrival at the gate in Miami, the connecting city, carries a feeling of relief. It is a strange sensation: coming home, yet not knowing what home actually is. In the terminal, travelers appear to be rushing through life, and even when I'm shoved aside by a woman in a hurry, I just smile. They are pressing towards solutions and business meetings and vacations, and they are oblivious to where I have been. The vendors in the airport are busy selling sandwiches, coffee, and sweet-smelling perfumes, and any luxury that can fit in a carry-on.

I move with the throng towards customs, past the plate-glass wall that separates us from the airplanes outside. The airplane I have just left is suspended on the tarmac, its massive engines shut down. I push towards the window, pressing my nose against it while the passengers whisk past. The silver skin of the aircraft sparkles, reflecting the midday sun, and below it the tarmac is lively. The bags progress down the rolling conveyor one by one and are retrieved by two burly baggage handlers who toss them over their shoulders simultaneously, in a game they have practiced before. The pilot steps onto the platform of the jetbridge and descends the stairs, taking a slow deliberate walk around the plane.

I place my palm against the hot glass, fixated, as one more pilot appears on the tarmac, then another and another until there is a line of them and the tarmac is dotted with dark suits. A woman who could be the widow stands in front, each of her arms braced by a pilot. Another moves slowly down the long line of men, handing each one a single white carnation. They stand like a valiant army, salute the airplane, and everything stops. There is no activity on the tarmac; all movement has ceased. The men remain still and silent, standing in a rigid salute as the conveyor belt begins to roll. There are no passenger bags. At the top of the conveyor a long container appears, preparing to make its way down. The men face it, united in a last good-bye to their comrade. The box moves slowly in a sad roll down the belt until it reaches the bottom, where six somber pilots step forward and gently lift it, placing it onto an electric cart. It is large and heavy, and stamped with the words *Jim Johnson*.

# chapter twenty-two

# Debrief

I have come to learn that when a commercial airplane crash occurs and the Emergency Response Team is activated, it marks the beginning of a domino effect that quickly takes on a life of its own. It begins with the team members, a group of people who possess no special skills in the area of psychology, who soon find themselves thrust into situations as traumatic as any on earth. The team members have not been trained in fitness or survival skills and have no knowledge at the beginning of who they will be at the end. As the domino effect continues, the team members establish contact with the survivors and the victims' families, who then contact their own extended families all across the nation, passing along details about the tragedy as it unfolds. In the end, when the dust settles, everyone is changed.

It is seven days after my return to Dallas when I enter the debriefing room and find a seat in one of the plastic chairs arranged in a circle. The mandatory debriefing has been prearranged, scheduled for a small group of local Emergency Response Team members. The sessions will continue for the next six months, held in various locations throughout the country, and this one will be held in a stark room at terminal C in the Dallas Fort-Worth International Airport, a room normally reserved for VIPs connecting to their flights. The room is surprisingly sterile and gray, with a circle of aluminum chairs arranged in the center. The walls are bare.

I select a chair nearest the door, watching the others congregate by the pot of coffee, in search of available mugs. There are six of us in the room, four women, all airport employees working at the ticket counter or in the airport operations group, identifiable by the navy-blue uniforms they wear. There are also two men; one wears the uniform of a flight attendant, the other is a bulky man in green tracksuit. He moves towards me and pulls the back of the empty chair until it is free enough from the circle to allow him to slide in. He glances in my direction and smiles, his eyes beaming with curiosity and light, ready for this adventure. He is forty or so, but his face exudes child-like warmth.

"This seat taken?" he asks.

"Of course not. Be my guest."

He settles in and places a bundle of jangling keys, sunglasses, and a small notebook on the floor beside him. The facilitator walks to the front of the room, her bluntly cut hair swaying across her shoulders. She introduces herself as Nancy Green, a psychologist employed by the airline's employee-assistance department, and requests that each of us introduce ourselves, one by one. The room turns silent, the awkwardness settling like snowflakes. We are about to be propelled into reality, reminded of the reason we are here.

I have had a week off from work already and now face a second week. The time away has been positive and I have not thought of the crash, nor Cali, or anything involving the tragedy. I have been shopping, running errands, and organizing closets, but I have not read the newspaper or taken calls.

When the introductions are over, we have all given our names and official titles. Nancy places a chair at the perimeter of the circle and tells us about the employee-assistance program, the area of the company responsible for handling drug and alcohol addiction rehabilitation and emotional-assistance programs for our employees. If an employee is proactive in seeking assistance for an addiction or emotional need, Nancy explains, he or she is entered into a confidential rehabilitation program and given time off from work to participate, and the program will negotiate all of it with the employee's manager on behalf of the employee. Although I have heard of the programs the department offers, I have been fortunate not to need one.

"My role here will be to help walk each of you through the emotional process following a crash activation," Nancy says. "The stress of an activation affects everyone differently, and although it's possible you won't experience anything negative, it's important to talk through the possibilities."

I know from the manual that post-traumatic stress disorder is a common aftereffect in crisis workers. It is an elevated form of depression consisting of nightmares that can be repetitive in nature and flashbacks containing the events surrounding a crash activation. The company might recommend a treatment program for the employee, or resort to an outside psychologist who could provide ongoing emotional counseling and support.

In addition to emotional afflictions, I also know that divorce rates among crisis workers are higher in general and that it is not uncommon for one who had worked a serious tragedy to become involved in an addiction of some sort afterwards. Drugs, alcohol, obsessive behavior, depression.

"It's important to monitor how you are responding to individual stresses," Nancy explains, "and equally important to keep a close network of family and friends at hand so that you have someone to turn to and talk things out with."

On the plane to Cali, I had read the section in the manual titled "Deactivation." It explained how Emergency Response Team members often find themselves embarking on a new career path after working a plane crash, or isolating themselves from their personal relationships, internalizing their feelings about the event. Most of the people I have met on the Emergency Response Team seem to have become even more loyal to the airline during the activation. Being put in the position to defend the airline daily against attorneys, media, and outsiders had a way of strengthening the bond, creating a group of insiders impervious to any flaws that were visible before. With the exception of Julie, I expect that most of the people I worked with during the activation will remain with the airline for as long as the airline will keep them.

Nancy leans forward in her chair, resting an elbow on a crossed knee. The mood in the room has lightened, mainly due to her casual demeanor and the way the chairs have been put together in an intimate, nonthreatening setting. I notice this, and also that there are no papers or forms here, just a small group of team members chatting in a circle like friends around a fire. The format has been planned, I suspect, years in advance. Nothing would be left to chance, and the important task of debriefing employees who had been privy to the innermost nuances and mechanics of a tragedy would be considered a top priority. In any crash, lawsuits are almost guaranteed and always expected. It would be critical to remain connected with the Emergency Response Team members who had been in close contact with the families of the victims. And if an emotionally unstable team member went on a destructive rampage a month after returning home from a crash site, the resulting press would be devastating for the airline. For a minute, I wonder if our answers are being recorded, but decide that I'm being far too cynical.

"Let's begin with a question about the activation," Nancy says. "The question is, How do you feel now about the work you performed during the activation? Do you feel as if you have helped or do you have feelings of sadness and regret? Or possibly a mix. There are no incorrect answers, by the way."

I remember the girl in the airport, the one who was sent home for displaying her true emotions. I search my mind for a short, uninvolved answer and pray that I am not the first one called on.

Nancy gestures to the woman closest to her, a thirty-something Dallas-based flight attendant with translucent skin and fine, delicate bones. She sits motionless for a moment as if to digest the question and find something meaningful to say. She purses her lips, which are lined in regulation red, a shade of lipstick within the allowable spectrum of colors selected by the airline. If a flight attendant is caught wearing a nail or lipstick color that is not within regulation, she will be warned, and a note will be placed in her file.

"I'd say I feel a mix of things," the flight attendant says. "In one way I'm sad—who isn't. But I also feel a sense of accomplishment because I am blessed to have been able to help others through a terrible tragedy." Her hands tremble and she knots them together in her lap.

The psychologist waits to see if there is more, but there isn't.

"Very good, thank you."

The male flight attendant is next and his answer is brief. He has worked two activations in the past, both minor, but events that prepared him to work with frantic family members. He'll be fine, he says, and will continue talking through the sad memories with a friend.

Everyone takes his or her turn answering the question, and soon I am next in line. The man beside me is up. He stares at his hands and mumbles his response.

"I've got a wife," he says sadly, "and two great kids, but I never really knew how much I loved them until now." He lifts his chin. "And I never knew that being activated would be so terrible." His eyes well and he rubs them with the back of a fist. "I'm a lifer, worked on the ramp over fifteen years now. But I don't care to work another plane crash, I'll tell you that."

The stillness is heavy. I fidget in my chair. When it is my turn to talk, I allow no time to pass.

"It was challenging, but I'm happy that I had the opportunity to help others. I feel very good about the whole process."

It is far less than I really feel, but my feelings have been pressed down so far that I could not retrieve them even if I wanted to. I will try not to relive the sadness. It will not be easy.

The instructor is satisfied. She nods and moves on to the next question, which revolves around the subject of victim identification syndrome, a problem associated with crisis workers who have worked closely with survivors and their families. Victim identification occurs when a crisis worker has become *too* involved, and manifests itself in the form of depression, anxiety, and distressing thoughts about the traumatic event. Our Emergency Response Team training had focused on remaining emotionally distanced from the victim's family members and now I understand why.

"I definitely identify with the family I worked with," answers Denise, a gate agent in Dallas. "I just can't stop thinking about the despair all these people have to live with now. Some of them lost their whole *families*."

As the session continues, I cannot help but remember a fascinating tale written by Thornton Wilder, called *The Bridge of San Luis Rey*, about a popular bridge in Peru that collapsed one afternoon, plunging five travelers to their death. The novel, which won a Pulitzer Prize, contemplated not the random event of the bridge collapsing, but the larger, philosophical meaning behind it. In the book, the main character attempts to understand why such a tragedy has occurred, and what qualities each victim might have possessed that would seem to link them to the same fate. It seems an insatiable quest, the journey to understand what cannot be understood. Yet the answer appears at the end of the novel, and it is an answer that satisfies all of my questions about the plane crash. A character in the book concludes:

> Soon we shall die and all memory of those five will have left the earth, and we ourselves shall be loved for awhile and forgotten. But the love will have been enough; all those impulses of love return to the love that made them. Even memory is not necessary for love.

There is a land of the living and a land of the dead and the bridge is love, the only survival, the only meaning.

The last sentence sticks in my mind. *There is a land of living and a land of the dead and the bridge is love, the only survival, the only meaning.* The bridge is love. For what else is there?

After more than two hours, we are finished and free to go. It is the last time I will reflect on my time in Cali, a time when I had the opportunity to help ease the suffering of others. Looking back, I am not convinced that I helped anyone at all. More than anything, I believe that we were there to keep the process in motion, by getting bodies back to the United States, completing paperwork, and running errands.

The first thing I had done upon arriving home was to empty my suitcase on the floor and remove the journal from Colombia, stuffing it into the far depths of a bookcase. In the ensuing weeks there will be forms to fill out, expense reports to submit, and a tactical log to complete that will detail any activities I performed during the activation. I will do all of it gratefully, because I have been on the other end of the tragedy. I was not a victim, and I have been granted another day. There will be things I am certain I will never forget, but for now I will try to leave everything about the crash behind me.

# chapter twenty-three

# The Ripple Effect

"Words cannot express my gratitude to you for your heroic efforts in the aftermath of the tragedy."

—*Director, Emergency Response Team*

The letter arrived two months after the crash, on company letterhead.

*Dear Tammy,*

*I doubt if you will ever forget the days that you worked the crash activation in Latin America. In my almost thirty years in the airline industry I have come to know quite a bit about our company and its people. I have learned that when our team understands a problem or a challenge, they respond and do what is necessary to deal with the situation. You and your colleagues on the Emergency Response Team certainly demonstrated this in response to the terrible tragedy. You were unselfish in your response, especially during the long and difficult days that followed. You can take great pride in helping people that needed your skill.*

*Please accept my personal thanks for being there when we needed you. We all hope and pray that we will never have another aircraft accident during our careers. I know that I can count on you to step up if needed.*

*Thanks again and Godspeed to you and your family.*

The letter was signed by a senior official of the company.

*  *  *

In the years that passed, I was fortunate to never work another activation again. I had kept the memories far away, held in a place in the past with all the other memories that I did not wish to excavate. The journal remained in a bookshelf in my brother's closet until I found it again many years later and tucked it into my briefcase. After the crash, my travel did not cease. I flew to countless destinations and logged hundreds of thousands of miles. Some days I traveled on four or five airplanes, shuttling from one meeting to the next, and back home again. I accepted another promotion, and life grew even more hectic as I traveled the country to meet with the sales managers who worked for me. One, a driven young woman whose abilities would earn her a fifty-thousand-dollar commission that year, approached me one day about the Emergency Response Team.

"I had heard you were on the team that went to Cali," she said excitedly. "I've been thinking about volunteering for the program and going through the training class. What do you think?"

The breath drew out of me. I hadn't thought of Cali in a long time.

"I think you've got a lot on your plate," I said, knowing that she would forget about it and move on to the next thing. "But it's up to you."

*  *  *

At times there would be stories on the crash, followed by articles on the litigation, then more accounts of the laws that had changed since the airplane went down. I ignored them, turning the pages of the newspaper to another section, keeping the past in the past. Months later, I heard from a team member that the analysis and subsequent reexamination of the results of the pilot specimens had shown that the alcohol that was detected on the pilot's body was derived from post-mortem microbial action, not from pre-mortem alcohol inges-tion. The bottom line was that any alcohol in the bodies of the crew was irrelevant and had not been a factor in the crash. The cause of the crash was determined to be myriad small details that, when added together, created a deadly outcome. The pilots had seemed confused by the in-flight computer system and became lost in the night after the wrong coordinates were displayed. They were con-fused about the location of the Cali airport, and radio communica-tion with the control tower could not clear it up. By the time the pilots understood that they were really lost, it was too late. The plane crashed into the mountain.

The journal from Cali eventually found a new home on my book-shelf, where it gathered dust until I opened it to write a story on one of the blank pages about a woman I had met on a plane. I had met so many people while traveling, and the miracle of flight did not leave me. In-flight, it seemed, people were devoid of inhibitions. They would talk about their most personal thoughts, sharing every-thing with a total stranger. On one flight, I met a woman whose only son, an airline pilot, had called her one day about a tingling sensa-tion he felt in his fingers when he awakened one morning. A doctor's visit found a brain tumor, and his demise was quick. Shortly there-after, she lost her husband, and she left me with a profound lesson about life and love: *Do it all now,* she had said. *Don't wait until it's too late.*

I knew that already, but even after the divorce and tribulations that followed, I spent too much time worrying, as we all do, and not enough chasing dreams. On another flight, I met a boy named Bax-ter, a teenager who had just lost his father in an airplane crash. And there were many others after them. On a flight to London I met a gruff, middle-aged attorney who could recite *Othello* with ease. There was the overweight, unkempt, shrimp salesman who I prayed would not have the seat beside me, but did, of course, and proceeded to explain to me the business of shrimp during the entire flight. He smelled like shrimp, he talked enthusiastically about shrimp, and his fingers were callused from handling shrimp. But by the end of the flight, I had learned more about shrimp and life, and prejudging people who seem different, than ever before. He was an interesting man who loved his work and his kids, and I have never missed an opportunity to talk to someone really different since then.

The miracle of flight has marked my soul with people and places that have forever changed me. I recorded all of these stories throughout the years, but it was not until recently that I read the journal from Latin America again, unearthing the contents and memories in its pages. It was then that I finally understood how true it is that everyone processes tragedy differently. Immediately following the crash, I had loathed the Emergency Response Team members who had bared their souls during the debriefing session and dwelled on their grief. They were weak, I had thought. But their grief was at the surface, and they dealt with it all at once. I, on the other hand, had chosen to ignore it, to act as if nothing had affected me. It had, but I did not acknowledge it for years.

# chapter twenty-four

# A Survivor

In Cali, the days flowed into one another. Amidst the assignments we were given was the endless wait for updates on the condition of the survivors and hopes that more would be found. When I scan through the journal years after, I remember how each day was unpredictable. There are notes outlining moments and tasks I cannot recall, as if someone else had lived them, and I have decided to transform them into a book about the crash and the people who volunteered to give their time during the activation.

The journal has brought back memories of the events surrounding the crash, making it impossible to purge the image of the little boy whose parents died from my mind. For reasons I cannot explain, it has become important for me to know how his life has turned out and to understand how he and the other survivors have fared. Did the boy spend his life surrounded by a loving extended family? Or has he suffered? Perhaps I will never know. Have the crash survivors been able to get past the tragic events of one single day that changed their lives forever? I have been unable to move beyond these questions, as if answering them will allow me to understand the meaning behind the tragedy and bring it full circle.

So I searched out the telephone number for Mercedes Ramirez, though I could not explain why I felt so drawn to her and not the others. From the moment I first saw her picture, something wedged inside my heart. She had been young, like me, with the rest of her life ahead of her. But in one single moment she lost her parents and almost her life, becoming an orphan, a victim of tragedy, a survivor. Perhaps I identify with her because I too had been touched by tragedy when my own father committed suicide, and I know that she will never again experience the innocence of pure abandon—that moment where one laughs deep from the gut, head back, mouth open, eyes lit up. She would laugh again, yes, but it would be eventually be interrupted by a memory. The eyes would darken and the laugh would grow softer, and others would see that deep inside, something heartbreaking had branded her soul. I had found it impossible to define this feeling for anyone who had not experienced tragedy, for only those who had suffered the loss of a child or been marked by trauma too young could understand. It is the difference between experiencing the world blind and deaf, or experiencing it with all of your senses. The world is still there, but it is different.

Throughout the years, I had been unable to get Mercedes out of my mind, and after reading the journal I made a decision. I would search out her number and call her, and if possible, I would meet with her. Yet even as I became convinced about this decision, I was occupied with doubt. Was I attempting merely to understand the philosophical meaning behind the event, like the character in the novel *The Bridge of San Luis Rey*? Would meeting a survivor be a meaningful experience, or a selfish one? I had nothing prepared to say to her when I picked up the telephone and dialed.

In our brief telephone conversation to arrange the visit, Mercedes asked few questions and insisted on picking me up at the airport in Kansas City, where she now lived. Her demeanor on the telephone was friendly and disarming, and my mind raced with questions. Why would she agree to talk with me? After all, five years prior I was a part of what stole her life and her innocence away. How had the years treated her? It had been eighteen long hours before they found her on the mountain. Did she believe in God? Had she believed before? I did not know the answer to anything, except that Mercedes Ramirez was a survivor.

I made the decision to take the short flight to Kansas City, where Mercedes worked as a sales representative in the healthcare industry. We would meet and talk over dinner, though I was uncertain about exactly what we would talk about. I had pondered the events of that day five years ago so many times, but always pushed it from my mind. The incident, as I had been trained to call it, was like a shark prowling the ocean floor, and I was a wader in the water above. It was large and ominous, its jaws unforgiving, and it would creep into my consciousness in unpredictable ways. The dark eyes of the Hispanic child in the grocery aisle, the taste of plantains at an upscale Manhattan restaurant, and always, without fail, on Christmas. I'll never shake that Christmas in Colombia or the image of the brilliantly decorated tree that towered inappropriately in the center of the hotel lobby where grieving family members huddled. I stood there for hours by that tree to greet them, and each time it was the same. First, the ding of the elevator bell, followed by a swell of sad, defeated faces spilling out of the cramped vessel to the base of the tree. That image would return at the sight of every hotel Christmas tree thereafter, and the sound of any elevator marking its landing. Yet those memories would be the good ones. There are others.

I pace the unfamiliar airport sidewalk waiting for her and the questions roil in my head. What will she look like? Will she look the same? How will she feel about meeting me?

When she pulls up in her sports utility vehicle and parks at the curb, my anxiety disappears. She extends her hand and offers a warm smile, and though I am uncertain where this meeting will take us, I know without question that fate or something beyond it connected us long ago.

"How was your flight?" she asks, pulling her seat belt across her chest. Her voice is soft and measured.

She is wearing a business suit, with a dainty strand of pearls encircling her neck and matching earrings. She is twenty-six now, married, no kids. Her hair is a thick cascade of curls, and she looks exactly as I remembered her from the photograph in Cali, only she is far more feminine than I would have imagined. It is just one of the qualities that sets her apart from other women her age.

"The flight was fine," I reply, aware of everything she has been through. "Nice and short."

It is a simple question, but when I answer I realize that maybe flying means something different to her. I wonder if she flies at all anymore, or even if she normally allows herself to be near the airport. These are questions I cannot ask, because it would be intrusive and rude to ask them, but I wonder nonetheless.

We drive to get something to eat. Inside the restaurant, the dinner crowd begins to gather and my stomach turns nervously. The hostess leads us to a table. Mercedes moves steadily and gracefully, like a dancer. I watch her as she peruses the menu, and I draw it all in. She turns the page of the menu delicately, then places it on the table to examine it. When she looks up, her eyes flicker over my face. They are oversized almonds, with exceptionally long lashes, and reveal nothing of what she has been through.

"So what made you want to contact me?" she asks.

"I'm not sure. I just felt like I had to know you, to somehow reconnect. I'm no longer with the airline, like I said on the phone. I write now, and I've written a book about the *incident*, which I suppose has stirred up all kinds of memories."

"That's understandable."

She is polite and kind, like the family I had been assigned to in Cali. And she is professional and polished, just as I had been when I worked for the airline.

"I didn't know if you'd want to meet with me," I reply. "Is there anything that you'd like to ask me? About myself, or about things that you haven't resolved yet in your mind, about the event?"

"Well, not really. Maybe though."

A flashback streams through my mind and I am taken back to my very last assignment during activation. I had just watched the pilot's body roll down the conveyor and was frozen to the glass for several minutes. After that, I walked numbly through the terminal and passed through customs, where I was greeted by another airline employee who handed me a walkie talkie and asked me to stand guard beyond the customs area where the electric doors open into the airport terminal, leading out to the curb. Reporters were waiting there with lights and cameras, ready to question the family members as they arrived home. I remember how I had approached the reporters and pushed them away, outside of the airport terminal, so the victims' families could safely pass, and how angry I felt at their intrusion. At the time I had felt protective of the families; in some ways it was the same feeling I felt now.

We are interrupted by the waitress, who takes our order. Mercedes orders a small rack of ribs, and I order a steak and a large baked potato. When the waitress disappears, we make small talk, covering the basics about our lives since the crash. In the time that has passed, Mercedes has gotten married to the young man she met just a month prior to the accident. She has recovered from her injuries to lead a normal life and has conducted speaking engagements about her experience from time to time. She is eloquent and well spoken, and I can clearly see how she could be an inspiration to others who have been through tragedies. As we talk further, I can see that helping others is one of her life's goals.

"What did you do while you were there?" she asks.

"Several things. Basically anything that was asked of me. I was assigned to help a family who lost someone in the crash, and I also helped with various administrative tasks."

"Did you see me or the other survivors? Did you come to the hospital?"

"No. But we received updates on your condition on a daily basis. We were all excited when we learned you would be okay."

"My sister was in the hospital with me," she says, smiling. "She helped keep the media away from me and she basically took care of everything. She was great. But they told us we could not bring our parents back to the United States."

Her eyes well, and I fight the same feeling as before, when I sat with the little boy at the table in Cali, fighting emotion. I had worked on the process of returning passengers to the United States, but I do not know what happened with her parents. I can only assume that they were not shipped because of the condition of the bodies, or that somehow there had been a misunderstanding.

"There must be a reason," I say, fumbling with words.

Fragments return to me and I remember the Dallas command center, packed with emotionally drained, sleep-deprived airline employees. They had erupted in cheers like football fans witnessing a touchdown the moment Mercedes was found.

"Do you remember anything from that day?" I ask.

"Yes, I remember that I was sitting by my mother, and my father was seated in a row behind us. When the movie came on, it was *Die Hard* with Bruce Willis, I think. I went and switched seats to I could sit with my father to watch it."

I nod and listen.

"It was my birthday that day and the trip had been part of my gift. I had been to Colombia many times, but not at Christmas."

I know the rest. On December twentieth, they boarded the flight that would change everything. As I sit across from her, I am overcome with the notion that we will be friends forever. We are still strangers, but somehow I know that we will forever be linked in a meaningful way.

Part of me believes that I have come here because I feel guilty, though there is nothing for me to feel guilty for. I did the best that I could, but now I believe that even my very best, at that age, could be beneficial to no one at all, and had the potential to do more harm than good. Another part of me reasons that if I could see Mercedes, the survivor, I would have closure, because I would know that everything was all right, and that everything happens for a reason. It is something one hears frequently throughout their life, yet I have searched my mind and the reason for the crash evades me.

"I was unconscious for a long time, and when I woke up I was on the ground, on the mountain, and I don't think I remember much except that Mauricio was there. He had been walking around for quite some time, not unconscious but alert, so he saw so much more. It was so much worse for him…"

Her voice trails off. She looks down and shifts the napkin in her lap. I push away the image of a mountain littered with bodies, some whole and ejected from their seats, others completely dismantled. Mauricio would have witnessed it all, and I can only imagine the shock of the silence, after everything had stopped moving.

"The next thing I remember is waking up in the hospital," she said. "My sister came in from the United States. The nurses were all being very gentle to me, but so cautious. No one would tell me what happened to my parents."

She speaks softly and her eyes dim.

"I think a reporter finally blurted it out," she says sadly.

I shake my head at the horror of learning such news by someone with only a banal interest in the tragedy.

"That's terrible," I say.

Mercedes shrugs and changes the subject. "Have you contacted the other survivors?"

"No. Just you. Do you keep in touch with them?"

"Yes, once in while, though I think the media invasion was too much for a lot of them. Mauricio was really resentful of the media at the time."

She takes a sip of the soda on the table in front of her.

She has excelled in her career in the healthcare industry, receiving several promotions over the course of her time in the corporate world. She travels frequently and works with doctors and executives all over the nation. The only evidence I find of what she has been through comes when I least expect it, as I lean over to retrieve my napkin from the floor. Even as I first see it, it comes like a slow-motion film, and I am taken aback. We are laughing, and the napkin slides to the floor. I lean sideways, beneath the table, and as I glance down to pick it up I see the scar. It is a small burn mark, a scar that peeks out from beneath her black leather pumps. I stop laughing, because the scar reminds me that there is so much more.

# chapter twenty-five

# Moving Forward

In the weeks that follow our initial meeting, Mercedes and I stay in touch, exchanging emails and telephone calls. It is during one of these conversations that I discover fate has touched us again: Mercedes's husband has accepted a coaching job in the Dallas area with a college basketball team, and soon they will move to the city where I live.

On the summer of their arrival, Mercedes calls for lunch, giving me directions to the hotel where they are staying. It's an efficiency-style complex in a decaying part of the city, a stopping point for sales reps and businessmen who plan to be in town for more than a few nights. Each unit has a kitchen where the guests can prepare their own meals.

"Be forewarned," she says. "It's not the best hotel in town. I booked it over the phone."

It's 11:30 in the morning on a Wednesday when I get into the car to head across the city to meet her. My farmhouse looms large in the rearview mirror as I pull away on the gravel drive, and the four dogs bark ferociously from the edge of it, tails wiggling uncontrollably. I make my way down the country lane that circles back around my property to the highway and get one more glimpse of the house I had bought the previous year, when I left my career in the airline industry behind. It is a grandiose Victorian jewel among the smaller, boxy homes that line the street, and the fifty-year-old old barn by the pond had lured me in from the moment I first saw it. I was ready for a change and I had thought at the time that even if the house weren't there I would be content to renovate the barn and live in it, like a poet.

In the year since I had purchased the property, many had tried to convince me to tear the barn down and start over.

"Sure would be cheaper just to tear it down and put up one of those buildings," said the ranch hand I had hired to renovate. He pointed to the rectangular aluminum buildings my neighbors had erected: oversized, hangar-like structures on large cement slabs.

"No," I had insisted. "I want to restore it to its original condition."

Twenty miles down the highway, I find myself thinking about Mercedes and the home they're building on a golf course in an exclusive neighborhood. There have been other exciting changes in her life, including a career move that will allow her to work from her house in Dallas.

I pull into the parking lot of the address she has given me and find a space in front of the hotel, which resembles an old apartment complex. There is no identifiable lobby and I consider ringing her on my cell phone, but in minutes she appears, zipping around the corner in a teal Jaguar. I lock up my car and get into hers for the short drive to the restaurant.

The conversation is light between us, now that we have moved beyond the initial tragedy that connected our lives. The crash remains vivid in my mind during every encounter we have, and though we are settling into a normal friendship, I still find it hard to be with her and be *fully* with her, without thinking about all she has been through. I know I am doing her an injustice when I surround us in the past, yet even when I set my mind to the task of forgetting how we are connected, something intrudes. An airplane circles in the sky, and I remember how she had been motionless in the hospital, and how the reports on her and the condition of the other survivors streamed into the command center on a daily basis. Critical, stable, fair. *Released.*

There is so much I want to ask about the crash, yet the fact is that none of it matters at all. So I do not ask, although there are times when she offers, and other times when it seems she just needs to tell me certain things.

The restaurant she has chosen is a small barbeque joint, packed to capacity, with photographs of celebrities covering the walls. The lunch crowd is a mixture of cowboys in hats and starched wranglers and executives with cell phones and Palm Pilots next to their plates.

"Flying doesn't bother me," she announces, settling into a chair at the table the waitress has led us to. I had summoned the courage to ask her this in the car, because she has flown several times since we met. She is constantly in the air, in fact, for business travel, and I sense that she is not the kind of person to let one tragic day define her.

"Sometimes it bothers me," I admit. "But it never did before."

I do not have to explain what I mean by "before," because she knows exactly what I mean. We talk of the accident without really mentioning it, which I have since learned from various therapists is quite normal. Those who have experienced a tragic event often do not talk of it, and if they do it is referred to in subtle ways.

"Did you always believe in God?" I ask, noticing the small cross she wears.

It would be understandable to me if she had no faith at all after the tragedy she had been through, and also understandable if her faith had grown stronger.

"Yes," she replies without hesitation. "I believe in God. My parents instilled that in us."

I envision a house filled with rosaries and images of Mary, the kind of Catholic upbringing that I had seen in many homes in Latin

America. She had been raised in the United States, but her parents were tied to their roots. One thing I knew for certain about many Hispanic families was the way they forged together in tragedy and the way each family tended to be much closer than the average American family. It was not uncommon for the mother and father and grown children to live in the same neighborhood, and some would live together under one roof even after the children had gotten families of their own. Their dinners and holidays would be massive, with every extended family member attending. In my opinion, they had their priorities in the right place.

We eat quickly and fight over the bill. By the time we are back in the car, we have made a joint decision: Mercedes and her husband will come to live with me during the next thirty days until their new home is complete. The hotel, she admitted, had felt scary for her when Chris, her husband, had left on an overnight business trip. Recruiting season was underway and his trips would be more frequent as he traveled the country looking for new basketball players for Southern Methodist University, the college team he worked for. Mercedes would feel more comfortable at my house, which would be big enough for us to coexist without getting in each other's way. I am excited about the prospect of having her there.

A month later, after we have emailed each other daily, sometimes even from opposite ends of the house, I cannot help but feel as if it was all predestined. I sit in my study at the antique desk and write for hours on end, surrounded by trinkets from Colombia: the beetle from Buga, nearly three inches in diameter and encased in a small Plexiglas grave; the Colombian currency; and the photograph I took from the airplane window as I returned home. I have a lesson to learn from Mercedes, although I suspect it may be years before I truly understand what it is.

I did not remove any evidence of Cali when I invited her because I did not think of it until it was too late, and then when I did, it seemed too obvious. The one exception was the Emergency

Response Team manual on my credenza, which I was horrified to see there when I first took Mercedes and her husband through a tour of the house. I tossed a newspaper over it, not wanting to bring anything from the past to bear.

In the evenings, I smell the elaborate meals cooking in my kitchen, smells that are foreign to my home. Mercedes cooks spicy, traditional meals like her mother had, making dishes from Latin America that I have never heard of before. One night, the house smells like it had in the restaurant in Cali, and another night she makes a dish that smells better than anything I have eaten in my life.

Mercedes and her husband make an interesting couple, and I admit that if I didn't already know they were married, I'd never place them together. Chris is tall as a bear, a former college basketball player who's built like a linebacker. He is the quintessential all-American male, seeming most comfortable in college sweatshirts, shorts, and a ballcap. He is happiest in the living room watching ESPN, while Mercedes, in contrast, is happy to work quietly in the kitchen, responding with a smile to the jokes her husband tells from the other room.

I have come to learn that she believes wholeheartedly in a traditional marriage and the roles of husband and wife. She is unruffled when Chris returns home after one in the morning, after a night out with the boys.

"Aren't you angry with him?" I ask, only half-kidding. Chris is sprawled on the couch in front of the television.

"Angry, heck she gets her nights out with the girls," Chris calls to us.

"I trust him," she says, smiling. "He needs his time with the guys."

She is supportive, loving, and far more tolerant than I could ever be. She makes me feel as if I have a lot to learn, because she can easily put everyone else's feelings and needs above her own, even when she is saddled with meetings and the stresses of everyday life.

Nearly a month into our living arrangement, I arrive home to be greeted by Mercedes at the front door, cooking utensils in hand, the scent of a native Colombian dish wafting through the foyer. She has prepared an elegant dinner for me.

"Surprise!" she says, beaming. She is radiant.

I have pondered the qualities that Mercedes and the others possessed to make them survivors, but it is a question without an answer. Is it strength, knowledge, youth, or just fate? I have asked her, but she does not know. Three of the survivors were under twenty-five, one was not. Mercedes is strong, but she is afraid of everything: my dogs, bugs, and many things that are surprisingly small. *But she is not afraid of planes.* It seems to me that only God knows why she has survived. I have a strange theory that God seems to take those who are most ready, because I once read a news story about a man, sitting on the porch of his small house in the country, reading the Bible. A plane came from nowhere and crashed right into the house, killing him. It was a story that stuck with me forever.

Mercedes introduced me to her sister Sylvia over lunch one day at a Chinese restaurant overlooking an ice-skating rink in the center of the Galleria mall. Later, Sylvia wrote a note to me, explaining how everything in her life had been changed by the tragedy and how she had felt the moment she received the call that no one wants to get.

"You can never begin to imagine that tragedy can happen to you," she wrote. "Well, it can. I felt like Michael J. Fox in the movie *Back to the Future*, where he is looking at a picture where he's fading away because his past was not occurring the way he knew it had happened."

Sylvia said that she now tries to appreciate the small things in life, because those are the things she'll remember the most, the small things that she did with the ones she loves.

"Like the saying goes," she said, "think big thoughts, but relish small pleasures. I enjoy watching the trees change colors for fall, I enjoy just sitting on my porch watching a lightning storm go by. These are all God's gifts that we can share with our loved ones."

I read her words years after the crash and it hit me all at once. I realized in that moment that the meaning of life is so simple and that those who had seemed weak and uncomplicated to me in the past were really the strong ones, who held the world in their hands. The key to happiness is the ability to exult in the stillness of any moment, to be able to find beauty in something around you when the line is long and everyone else is growing angry and impatient. The secret to a wonderful life is to be grateful for every color, every season, and every smell, and to keep moving forward with faith when the tragedies strike, passing your wisdom on to those who follow.

"Life is precious," Sylvia wrote. "I try to instill that in my family, especially Nicholas, my son. God never gives you anything you can't handle. When my mom went with Dad, God did not leave me on this earth alone…he gave me my sister back. My sister has so many of both of my parents' characteristics, and she is my connection to the past."

\* \* \*

I continue to call Mercedes from the car and I call her from airports, and though we live beneath the same roof our conversations occur in electronic form or sound bites over the cellular waves far more often. When I see her she is always poised, a quality that sets her apart from everyone else. Even in flannel pajamas, there is an aura that surrounds her, a calm that settles the room when she enters.

I live on a private airport at the end of a runway, which is another ironic fact that escapes me until we are all standing there on the back porch overlooking the barn, with the airplanes circling overhead. *How could I be so stupid?* I think. How could I have invited her here, when each night the airplanes will buzz the house, which is positioned too close to the very tip of the runway? It is daunting for every first-time visitor, the sound of the pilots practicing their takeoffs and landings every night, buzzing so close to the rooftop that it seems they will crash through the upstairs bedrooms. And each day, Mercedes will have to travel the runway in her car, heading to appointments or the grocery store, and she will have to learn to pull over and wait until the airplane taxis by her car, because an airplane always has the right of way.

I stand on the deck and marvel at my stupidity while Chris turns the steaks on the grill. Mercedes brings him a cold beer and the three of us stand there, taking in the aroma while the sun sets into the valley, against a salmon-colored sky. It is an awe-inspiring moment, a night as perfect as any I've witnessed, and more than that it is a moment that is so *normal*, so wonderfully suburban from where we have been. But then, in an instant, the feeling changes.

I am the first to see it, I think, the airplane that spirals ominously towards the house. It moves fast in a downward spiral, not forward through the air in a glide. I tense up, because soon we can see every detail on the small red biplane, including the numbers on the side. It appears as if the pilot has lost control, and the silence on the deck turns awkward, until I feel naked and exposed to the reality that I did not contemplate any of this before.

We stand motionless on the porch for an eternity, and I hold my breath. Suddenly, the pilot jerks the plane out of the dive, soaring straight upwards into the sky. The biplane launches like a rocket towards the heavens and I can breathe again. But when I look at Mercedes she is calm, as if it had not bothered her in the least. She flashes a brilliant smile, and dismisses the antics of the pilot with a wave of her hand. In one gesture she relieves my discomfort, a trait I later learn was inherited from her mother, who would have done anything to make others feel at ease. Mercedes refuses to be a victim and insists on a life that is as normal as everyone else's. She will not let what has happened to her become an obstacle that prevents her from achieving a life overflowing with opportunity and success. *This*, I realize, is the quality that makes Mercedes a survivor.

There have been other survivors since, along with other airplane explosions and airplane hijackings, and even an incident involving a young woman who jumped to her death from the door of a corporate jet. It was the last one that stuck with me the most, like a shard of glass wedged in my heart. I clipped out the article, like I had done before, and tucked it into the back of my wallet.

Since then there have been earthquakes and shootings and deaths we cannot explain, and the tragic hijacking of four airplanes on September 11, 2001, that affected almost everyone in America. Lives all over the world have been touched by tragedy, and I no longer spend my time wondering why, or what it's all about, because it is more important to live.

For Mercedes, the memory of her parents is the answer, something I suspect she strives to keep alive each day. Though I never met her mother, I can see shades of her in her daughter: the cooking, the cultural attitudes she has inherited. Her mother is everywhere, and her father, too. For Mercedes, like the role model established by her parents, the greatest achievement of all would be a lasting and forever relationship, a marriage that produces happy children and a union that will last until the end of time. The man she met a month before the crash has stood by her through the desperate months after she was rescued from the wreckage, and now, as her husband. Once they are settled, she says, and firmly entrenched in their new careers, they will work on having children of their own. She tells me it is something she wishes her mother could be around to see, but she will do everything possible to make certain that her own children know who their grandparents were.

Mercedes is more than a wife or a sister or a daughter. She is an intelligent, magnetic force, someone who is constantly engaged in life. The coincidence or destiny of our coming together continues to intrigue me, as if it were a whisper from God. I have wondered how it feels for her to be so close to the heavens, to board that airplane again in the first place. I wonder if she thinks of it, and I wonder if she tears up or if she immerses herself in work to keep the walls erected around her. But more than anything, I have wondered how she can keep on flying, keep pressing the odds. The answer, I think, lies in that single day, when it seemed to be just another day and just another flight. To fly is to be where she was on the very last day that she saw her parents, to be close to that moment again.

Months later, after her house has been built and they are all moved in, Mercedes and I talk, and the strain in her voice is apparent. She has traveled for five days straight, calling on accounts on the West Coast.

"I'm actually tiring of all the travel now," she says. "So keep an eye out for me, will ya? If you hear of any jobs here in Dallas, let me know. I'd like to find something a little closer to home, stop pushing my luck, you know?" She adds a laugh to lessen the seriousness of the comment, but I understand. She does not want to travel much anymore, and who can blame her.

"Yes," I say. "I know."

# chapter twenty-six

# In Her Own Words

One day, six years after the tragedy, I ask Mercedes to write something that would capture her feelings about her parents. She wrote down her most vivid memories and sent them to me in the following story:

By Mercedes Ramirez Johnson, May, 2001

*Life has taught me many things during my relatively short time here on mother Earth. I have always thought that maturity and the sense of contentment in one's surroundings was a product of experiences, not age. The people that touch your lives, the friends that you make, the family that you have, and the events that transform your life all have an extraordinary impact on who you become and evolve to be. For me, my life has been a blessing. I have always been surrounded by loving parents, a caring sister, and wonderful friends. As I grew up, my nucleus was closely knit and I grew up thinking that everyone was surrounded by the same love. But during my junior year of college, my nucleus was shattered to pieces.*

*"Quien es la negrita mas linda del mundo?" my father would ask me as I sat on his lap.*

*Who is the prettiest negrita in the world?*

*"YO!" I would reply, with a big grin as I hugged him.*

*I don't know how many hundreds of times my father asked me that question, but it would always make me feel special, loved, and pretty. Negrita, roughly translated, is the affectionate way in Spanish of refer-ring to a person with dark skin. My sister, nine years my elder, has porcelain white skin compared to me, so my parents always referred to me as "la negrita." I took after my father.*

*When you are five years old and sitting on your dear father's lap, you never know where life is going to take you. You never know what obstacles will be thrown in your way, and you never know how strong of a person you are until you come face to face with death.*

*I grew up in a loving, hardworking family of four. My mother was from Nicaragua and my father was from Colombia. They had met some thirty years ago in Los Angeles, and a mere three months later they were married and ready to face the world in the United States, knowing little English, but with all the heart and desire for happiness in the world.*

*My parents came from hardworking families and always wanted my sister Sylvia and I to live by those examples. Above all else, my par-ents stressed to us the importance of an education. During the last ten to fifteen years of her life, my mother worked on the sanitation crew for a cookie manufacturer. She would come home tired and her hands would always look abused from the harsh chemicals she handled in her job. I remember one day when I was in high school my mother came home from work and took off her gloves to expose hands that were red and chaffed. She looked down at her hands and then looked at me with tears in her eyes.*

*"Never work with your hands, always work with your mind," she said.*

*My father always said that no matter what happens to me in the future, that no one would ever be able to take away my education. To this day, I live by those consejos, teachings, that they always tried to instill in me. As your typical kid, they probably thought it went into one ear and out the other, but I wish I could tell them how much I lis-tened and how many lessons I learned from them.*

*My mother, Mercedes Ramirez, was born and raised in Nicaragua. She came to the United States only knowing one friend of the family who lived in San Francisco. As soon as she arrived, she realized that the English she had learned in school got her nowhere, so she had to start from scratch to learn the language all over again. She always used to say that the English language is the hardest to learn—too many ways one letter can be pronounced.*

*My mother was always known as the life of the party. She knew exactly how to have a good time and thought it was important to make others feel comfortable and at ease, so they could have fun. Her sharp and witty sense of humor was her trademark, and one of her greatest gifts was making people laugh. My mother had silvery gray hair and smooth tan skin, and to this day, I've never met anyone with a complexion as beautiful as my mother's. She was also a very loving, helpful person, and I recall so many examples of how she expressed her compassion for those around her. If there was someone at her work who didn't have family around and was going to have a baby, my mother would throw them a baby shower. If someone we knew was in the hospital, we'd go and visit them after church. If there was a new Cuban family that had just arrived to the Kansas City area, my mother would help collect clothes for them.*

*When it came to raising money for the various Hispanic organizations and scholarship funds in the area, my mother would always be the first person called. She would sit on that phone for hours at a time gaining people's support for a benefit dance or a fundraising dinner. She would devote herself 100 percent to everything she did. My mother was an amazing woman, and I can only hope that one day when I have children they will say the same about me. I cannot do justice to her memory by describing her in words, but I will always have the memories, and will strive to be the kind of person she was.*

*My father, Benjamin Ramirez, was a strong yet gentle man. He was born and raised in Colombia, and his claim to fame was that for over twenty years he was a professional wrestler. He wrestled under a* number of different names, but one element remained constant—he was always the villain. He said he didn't want to be the "baby face," which was wrestling lingo for the good guy. Ironically enough, the villain suited him just fine because he had always been the scary, silent type, large and quiet. Only in real life he was the sweetest man, not scary at all. His most famous character during his wrestling years was the Mummy, or La Momia Azteca.

My father loved to share the hilarious stories of his wrestling days, about all the people he met throughout his career, the pranks they'd pull on each other while on the road, and the beautiful countries he visited while he wrestled. But the most important stories my father would tell involved my mother, and how they had built their family around that life. They had lived like Gypsies—my father, mother, and sister—traveling from one venue to another with all that they owned packed in the back of a trailer. It was a hard life, to live in one city for three months, then another for one year, then another for six months and on and on again. There were many wrestlers who just left their families in one city and would do all the traveling alone, visiting their families during the breaks. But my parents wanted to be together, so they chose the traveling.

My father was always known to be a true gentleman in every sense of the word. Even though he was tall and muscular, he was the most gentle and kind man you could ever meet, and I remember that he always had words of advice for his daughters. One of the things I miss the most about my father are his hugs. He would bear hug all of us and say, "Always remember this hug because the four of us here are all that we have."

He wanted us always to remain close to one another.

I have immortalized those memorable hugs for my sister in a custom-crafted pendant that displays four diamonds surrounded by gold, united on the top and bottom by sapphires. It has a special meaning. The diamonds, the strongest out of all the precious gems on earth, symbolize our small family. The top diamond is my father, the gold around the diamonds are his arms holding us together. The sapphires are among the second most durable gems in the world, and represent the bond of our family—strong and everlasting. It is a bond that nothing can take away. My sister wears her pendant every day.

My parents met in California. My father was in town for the weekend on a pit stop between wrestling trips to Japan, and his sister, who had a friend that was throwing a Father's Day party, invited another friend of hers—my mother—to stop by, too. My mother was enjoying the party until, as she told it, a tall, handsome man pulled up in a fancy car with sunglasses, and kissed my aunt. At the time my mother assumed that he was her friend's boyfriend, so she went back to her business at the party. But then my aunt introduced my father as her brother, and my mother went to work. As the music played, my mother started talking to my father and said that she loved the music but she wished she knew how to dance and enjoy it. But for those who know my mother, they know that it was the absolute farthest from the truth—my mother was born dancing! For the rest of the evening, my father "taught" my mother how to dance, even though years later he admitted he knew something was going on because she danced better than he did.

That next morning, he invited my mother and his sister to breakfast before his flight back to Japan. My parents exchanged addresses, and after three months of letters, postcards, and occasional phone calls, my father told my mother he had a contract to wrestle in Nicaragua. During the three-month period, his correspondence had been friendly yet never really romantic, but one day he asked my mother if he could pass by and visit her parents, because he wanted to ask them for her hand in marriage.

My mother was completely surprised, and she didn't know what to do! She liked him, but it had only been three months! She asked friends for advice, and one of them, who had known my father from Colombia, said that he had been a wonderful son and had treated his mother like a queen, and that men that are good to their mothers make *good husbands. So with that, my mother said yes, my father met the in-laws, and my parents got married. I guess times have changed because there is no way they would have let me marry someone I had known for three months. But love was strong in their marriage and I'm sure they are still in love to this day in heaven.*

*After I survived the airplane crash that my parents did not, my whole world changed. It was an experience that shattered my nucleus, but an experience that led me to value and appreciate life more than anything. My life was so close to being lost. I remember one day at the hospital in Kansas City when the attending nurse noticed that I was bored out of my mind. She decided to do something special for me, so after checking with my doctors and surgeons to make sure it was okay, she came into my room and told me I was going for a ride!*

*I had no idea what to expect when the nurse began her "prep" work, which involved securing my IVs, my illiostomy bag, and my catheter into place to ensure the wheelchair ride of the afternoon. After all my attachments were made mobile, I slowly went through the process of getting out of bed and into the wheelchair. The nurse loaded me up and pushed me slowly down the halls. It was nice to get out of my room and to actually be sitting straight up, because for months I had been in a hospital bed lying face up or on my side. My hospital room in the Intensive Care Unit was on one of the top floors of the hospital, so when I'd look out the window, all I could ever see from my bed was the sky.*

*The nurse took me to the skywalk and stopped there to let me look down on the streets below from my wheelchair. It was there that, for the first time since my parents' death and the plane crash, I saw life. I saw people bustling in their winter coats as the snow fell unto the slushy streets. I saw the rushed energy of visitors to the hospital, deliverymen, clinical staff, and cars rushing back and forth. And it was there as I sat in my wheelchair looking down to the street that tears rolled down my face.*

*"Are you okay?" the nurse asked, worried that there was something wrong.*

*I don't remember how I responded to her, but all I know is that watching life made me want so badly to get back into it. There are days now when I'm stuck in traffic or I get rained on without an umbrella, and instead of getting upset, I try to remember that day and that painfully strong feeling of loss that I had, from not being able to participate in life.*

# chapter twenty-seven

# Giving Back

In May of 2000, during a trip to Romania to work in orphanages, I was inspired to create a nonprofit organization that would assist homeless and abandoned children. I had been staying in the town of Brasov, a small city three hours from Bucharest, with cobblestone streets and ancient, decaying buildings built during the communist era. I had been in three orphanages that day, painting the walls, playing with the children and serving them lunch, and I was struck by the dark, institutional lives they lived; indoors, without sunlight, sports, or the playtime activities that children in other countries took for granted.

The smell of the children who had clung tightly to my neck lingered, and my scalp throbbed from the little boy who had yanked my hair hard in retaliation when I tried to put him down. My heart wrenched with despair at his fate; he was hostile and raw, so hurt and abandoned that any reaction from an adult would be worth receiving, even if it were a negative one. I understood too well the destruction of abandonment, the lasting aftereffects, and the feelings that would never go away. I had cried for him when I left that day, and for Elena, the little girl with the big haunting eyes, and because I was just like everyone else who went there to volunteer and then walked away, right back into a normal life, leaving all those children behind.

Some had grown up in the orphanage and had never even seen a car or a playground. The demand was highest for infants, so most of the older children would never be adopted. At seventeen, I was told, they would be released into the world to fend for themselves, after a lifetime of living behind four walls with stern caretakers who could not teach them skills to survive in society or provide them with emotional support.

When I tried to fall asleep that night, I could only see the little boy and Elena cramped in their cribs. Although Elena was seven or eight and her body was lithe and growing, she was subjected to the same sleeping conditions as the smaller children, a small crib placed on the floor of a room crowded with others. It had been too much for me, so I stayed awake through the night until I came up with a way to bring some small amount of joy to their lives.

The purpose of the organization would be to touch the lives of children who had been orphaned or abandoned, youngsters with turbulent pasts and uncertain futures. We would build playgrounds at the orphanages, so that the children would have a place to play. The caretakers at the orphanage could supervise the children while they played outdoors on swingsets, activities that would help build confidence and physical skills. Mercedes was the first person I thought of for our board of directors. Not only did she have much to offer, but she could identify with their loss.

*  *  *

Months after her move to Dallas, Mercedes and I find ourselves together in her husband's sports utility vehicle on the way to Waxahachie, a small town an hour and a half south of Dallas, where we have volunteered to spend a long day under the grueling Texas sun. We will build two swingsets for children who spend time after school at a center for underprivileged youth. Though neither of us have carpentry skills, we're ready for the adventure.

The caravan of cars filled with volunteers from our group slows to a stop in front of the address I've been given. The volunteers are young professionals, like us, who have donated their time to the cause because, after everything they've been given in life, it is time to give back. Most of them are from Dallas or Fort Worth, and among them are an engineer, a vice president, and a technical sales rep. The projects have been funded from the money I earned during my time with the airline, and have ranged from building swingsets to cleaning a gymnasium built for children living in a homeless shelter.

The address where we will build swingsets today is an empty lot on a narrow street, in a desolate neighborhood dotted with ramshackle houses. The only structure on the lot is an old gray trailer, which sits across from a small shanty with a crooked wood porch that someone has wedged up with concrete blocks. The street is vacant, absent of life except for the drumbeat of a boom box drifting from a blue house at the bottom of the hill. We park in the dirt near the trailer and step out of the car.

"Pretty scary, huh?" Mercedes says, though I am certain that it's just a comment and that no situation as simple as this one would scare someone who has been in much worse.

"Yes," I nod, scanning the street. "Probably not the greatest of neighborhoods."

From the moment we entered Waxahachie, it seemed a town devoid of promise, one in which those who do get out run as far as possible towards bigger dreams. One hundred fifty years ago it was thriving and prosperous, due mostly to the arrival of the railroad, and for much of its history the county was a leading agricultural center in Texas because of the fertile soil. It was a county that was known to produce high yields of cotton that were harvested during the late nineteenth and early twentieth centuries, back when cotton farms blanketed the rural areas and gins dotted the landscape. Compresses, oil mills, and cotton-related businesses popped up and profits soared, leading to a construction boom that built many of the towns' historical monuments.

But in the thirties the town went into a steep decline as cotton prices and demand dropped dramatically, dragging down the little community with it. There was no new construction, no new jobs, and no economic growth. Left behind was a strong history of a lost place and time, archaic but grand buildings left vacant in one square block of the miniature downtown, and a museum full of documentation on the slave culture that developed as a result of the cotton industry.

\* \* \*

We walk towards the trailer in search of Broderick Sargent, the man who has agreed to meet us to give us our instructions. Broderick is a former football player for the Dallas Cowboys, a monster-sized man with large hands and wide, rippled shoulders. His voice is intimidating, deep, and decisive, which I know from our initial phone conversation about the shelter. I had searched out his number after reading an article about his youth center in the Dallas newspaper, and from that I knew that he had settled in Waxahachie after retirement, shunning the glamorous city life that many other former NFL players had sought out. Here he was a hero, a former running back with the Dallas Cowboys with a direct link to fame. He attended the city-council meetings; he worked hard to build the community. Here he represented the promise of what they could be.

Mercedes and I circle the trailer towards the front, and when we round the corner a tiny black girl is standing square in the dirt lot, watching as if she had known we were arriving. She's about ten years old, with sneakers so worn her toes show through. Her stomach bulges under a faded pink T-shirt that seems two sizes too small, drawing attention to the beginnings of tiny breasts. When we approach, she does not smile.

"Hey, how ya doing today?" Mercedes asks. Her voice is soft and childlike.

The girl nods and shrugs. She stares at the ground. Suddenly I am aware of how we appear on the outside, two white girls in a brand-new car, new sneakers, new threads.

"Are you having fun today?" Mercedes asks. "Playing outside?"

The girl nods silently. She clasps her arms behind her back and squeezes, staring at the ground. I search for a mother, but there is no sign of anyone except for three older boys who have gathered in the street, watching us. The oldest has a bike.

"How old are you?" Mercedes persists.

The girl raises her head. Her eyes are mahogany colored, solid with no flecks of pigment or light. They are eyes that don't belong on this little body, I think, but someone who has seen at least thirty years.

"Eleven," she mumbles.

"Eleven? Wow, you're big for eleven." Mercedes smiles broadly. The girl just shrugs, but a grin begins to form.

"Well, we'll see you in a little bit," Mercedes says. "We're going to build a nice big playground for you today."

We move down the small concrete walkway leading to the trailer, and when I look back the girl is still rooted to the same spot, watching. Suddenly the door to the trailer flies open and a man in a T-shirt and athletic shorts bounds out and down the steps. He rushes forward with a surge of energy.

"Broderick Sargent, how do you do?" he says, smiling broadly. He thrusts out a hand and offers a firm grip. His forearms and biceps are rippled with muscles and the T-shirt strains against them. After we make our introductions, Broderick takes us to the playground site. "That's where the swingset will go," he says, pointing to the dirt. "One day we'll have grass there."

Mercedes and I survey the dirt lot. The others in our group are emptying tools from the trunks of cars and some carry large beams of wood on their shoulders. Two of the volunteers carry toolboxes containing wrenches, wood screws, and electric drills. Others have brought the brackets needed to hang swings and the kit containing parts needed to craft a swing for infants. The only hard part will be the labor.

"How many swingsets are you building?" Broderick asks.

"We can build two if you want," I reply. "We've brought enough lumber and tools for two."

"Absolutely, if you can do it. We've got a lot of kids out here with nowhere else to go. They will love to come here after school and play."

From where we stand, I can see a cluster of children inside the trailer door, some gathered around an old donated pool table and others eating sandwiches that Broderick's staff has provided.

"There's a reporter over there," Broderick says, gesturing to a thin man with a notebook. "He's interviewing my brother about our center for youth, but after he's done he'll talk with you about your organization." He paused and stared at the lot as if the swingset was already there. "We really appreciate what you're doing here," he said thoughtfully. "We'd like to buy your volunteers lunch today."

We tell him it's not necessary, but he insists and asks us what time. We all agree on noon, and Mercedes and I thank him.

The organization we have created is long overdue, sprung from an inner need to provide for others. Mercedes has willingly joined in, taking an active role in the planning of projects and construction of swingsets for children who have none of the luxuries that other children have. The first swingset built will bear a plaque bearing an engraved inscription in honor of her parents. It will be crafted by all of us using treated lumber designed to withstand the effects of time. On the swingset built for her parents, children will laugh and play. Mercedes will leave a legacy for her parents that will remain standing for years to come.

* * *

When the flight Mercedes and her parents had been traveling on that day entered Colombian airspace, the Cali control tower had to track the airplane's progress by hand. Radar coverage was unavailable, and the controllers used flight progress strips to keep track of airplanes. To further complicate the transmission of data, the controller did not speak English beyond basic aviation terminology and the pilots did not speak Spanish. The air-traffic controller later told investigators that there were no language difficulties in the communications he had with the flight crew, but he did state that some requests the pilot had made seemed to make no sense. He added that if he had known English better, he would have asked more detailed questions.

When I am with Mercedes, I think about little details that, if missed, can add up to tragedy. One thing missed, combined with another thing, until the cards come tumbling down. It was that way on December 20 six years ago, when several small factors and missed details converged to cause a plane crash. I am so close to the day when I will be able to be with her without thinking of what happened.

I had buried the tragedy for so long, and I had erased that time in Cali from my mind because I did not want to dwell on the sadness. I did not want to wonder every year at Christmas about the little boy who lost his family. I did not want such an innocent time to be tainted by tragedy and the feelings of sadness associated with all of the haunting faces from the lobby, the ones who would always remember the Christmas that changed their perspective and lives. But I have since learned that buried feelings will always surface and never when you think they will. You can push things away, but eventually you will have to confront what's inside. Being with her has allowed me to do this all at once, and I find myself experiencing moments of pure joy and flickers of awareness, as I realize that tragedy strikes us all, in one way or another throughout our life. It has helped me deal with my past, and to understand that if I keep one eye in the rearview mirror, then I am not really living at all. Sometimes there are no answers.

I turn to speak with Mercedes but she is gone. I find her moments later dominating the center of a basketball court that someone has donated. Small boys surround her, and she holds the basketball in one hand, high above them. They taunt and tease her, and she jerks to the side, swooping the ball in front of them in one motion, then up again. She lifts the ball gracefully into the air and releases it and it sails into the basket effortlessly.

"Yeah! Who you gonna mess with now?" she says, laughing.

The boys scream and scramble for the ball. A small one with diminutive features wrestles it away and runs to the far side of the court. I move closer and snap several quick pictures, capturing the moment.

"C'mon over here! Think you can handle some hoops?" Mercedes grabs the ball from the boy and tosses it in my direction.

"I can take you guys any day."

"C'mon then," she says, "Let's divide into teams."

At noon, after several games of basketball and hours building the playground, Broderick and his staff arrive with a cooler overflowing with cold drinks. A woman on his staff carries a large box of soft biscuits and chicken fresh from the oven. The smell is intoxicating, and we follow them inside the trailer, where Broderick leads us to a small room in the back, which he uses both as an office and also as a counseling room for troubled kids and their parents. He sits at the head of a rectangular table and directs us to take the chairs around it. We congregate there and ferociously dive into the chicken.

When we are done we file outside, bringing the cooler with the drinks with us. A group of children follow, the smallest of whom is a little boy of about seven named Dimitri, who has taken a liking to Mercedes. Dimitri picks up the hammer and begins to pound the ground with it.

"Be careful with that, honey, don't hurt yourself." Mercedes smiles and the boy grabs her by the legs in a hug. He lowers himself onto the drink cooler and stares up innocently.

"Can I have one?" he asks. He opens the top and peers inside, then closes it again. He sits on the cooler and crosses his arms.

"Of course you can," she says, grinning.

The other children are watching and soon there is a swarm around the cooler until the supply is gone. Dimitri grabs a can of orange soda and runs towards the swingset with a hammer.

"He told me he lives here with his grandmother," Mercedes says, following him with her eyes. "He's from Dallas, actually, but he had to move here because he doesn't know where his mother is."

"What happened to her?"

"Just took off, I guess."

"What about his father?"

"His father got shot. He said he's seen a lot of people get shot."

She is quiet for a moment and her gaze is focused on the little boy, who stands in the middle of the crowd of men and attempts to hammer a small nail into a piece of wood. The hammer is too large for his tiny body, and it takes all of his strength to lift it with both hands.

"Makes you realize how lucky we are," she says.

# chapter twenty-eight

# The Future of Emergency Response Teams

In the years since the accident, there have been endless court cases on the crash, a common occurrence after commercial airplane crashes, and just as many theories about the cause. Several of the cases have been filed by attorneys representing the families to pursue litigation against the airline, and others have been filed by the airline itself, seeking damages from Honeywell and Jeppesen Sanderson, the companies that manufactured and programmed the in-flight computer the pilots used during descent. Ultimately, there were several causes, not just one, that led the 757 to descend blindly into the mountain that night.

The Boeing 757 had strayed from its path, something everyone agreed upon. Colombian investigators reported that the pilots entered the wrong codes into the flight computer, sending the plane off course, and then failed to notice the error as they descended. The court case filed by the survivors and relatives of the passengers on Flight 965 centered on determining if the airline had expressed willful misconduct because under the Warsaw Convention, a law enacted in 1929 to establish liability limits, airlines would not be liable for any amount over $75,000 per passenger, unless willful misconduct could be proven. This was standard procedure, but critical in determining overall compensation, and though the trial was expected to be long, U.S. District Judge Stanley Marcus found the airline guilty of willful misconduct after just four days of deliberation. "The truth won in the end," said Mauricio Reyes, one of the four who had survived. He planned to move on with his life, continuing his education at the University of Miami.

Judge Marcus issued a 118-page summary judgment about the case. "Simply put," he wrote, "no reasonable jury could find that acts of the pilots of Flight 965, and in particular the pilots decision to continue their descent at night from a grievously off-course position in mountainous terrain, amounted to anything less than willful misconduct."

*  *  *

Years later, I review the Colombian crash report for what seems like the hundredth time and it seems doubtful to me that the pilots were concerned about anything but the flight. Obviously they weren't out to kill themselves, nor the passengers in the cabin, but it was evident that by the time descent for landing occurred, there was tension in the cockpit, as both the pilot and first officer attempted to get their bearings.

Alfonso Bonilla Aragon International Airport in Cali is a difficult approach located in a long, narrow valley surrounded by mountains extending to fourteen thousand feet. The airport sits at an elevation of 3,162 feet, with a hard-surface runway more than nine thousand feet long. At the time of the accident, the airport control tower operated twenty-four hours a day and controlled departing and arriving traffic on two runways.

The Boeing jet had completed a B-level maintenance check in November, just a month prior to the crash. The B check was a standard maintenance-system check that every aircraft received and it reported no anomalies. The captain and first officer were also current on their training, which included flight-simulator proficiency checks as well as training regarding security and hazardous materials, crew resource management, and international operations. The captain completed an important annual line check just weeks earlier on December 9th, accompanied by a Federal Aviation Administration check airman. Ironically, the test was administered on the exact same routing, and the exact same flight number, Flight 965 from Miami to Cali.

The Colombian accident investigation report determined that several factors contributed to the crash. The report noted that the pilots were using a complex computerized navigational system, and although both Captain Tafuri and First Officer Williams articulated misgivings several times during the approach, neither displayed the objectivity necessary to recognize that they had lost situational awareness. The plane veered off course, and soon it was too late to correct. Investigators for American Airlines said that Captain Tafuri thought that he had programmed the flight management system on board the Boeing 757 to fly to the Rozo coordinate near Cali, Colombia—but that the command he entered steered the plane toward Bogota, nearly 130 miles in the opposite direction. Both beacons have a similar one-character identifier on the flight charts, (R), but showed different identifiers in the flight-management database. American Airlines's chief pilot sent a letter to its pilots after the crash warning of the inconsistencies between computer databases and aeronautical charts that could lead to confusion. Although one judge had ruled willful misconduct in the Cali crash, it was the opinion of many that it wasn't just one factor, but a series of complicated and confusing details that led to the accident.

*   *   *

In the year following the Cali crash, the United States government implemented the Aviation Disaster Family Assistance Act, a mandate that establishes the National Transportation Safety Board as the agency to coordinate family activities after a major crash. The act allows for ancillary action on behalf of the airline after a disaster, but names the NTSB as the primary contact for the families and victims, a law that resulted from the protests of victims' family members who had lobbied for an organization that would act as a liaison between the families and the airlines after a disaster.

In the event of a plane crash today, the airline is still heavily involved in the post-incident family process, only airlines must now coordinate the family response activities through a single, governing organization. This ensures that specific procedures are followed and that each family receives critical information on their loved ones as expeditiously as possible. And even though this change in law is a positive step towards streamlining the emergency-response process, it's my belief that even more changes will occur in the years to come.

\*   \*   \*

Based on my experience on an Emergency Response Team, I believe that the current system, although exemplary in several areas, could be modified in others. Future airline Emergency Response Teams in general could make modifications to the characteristics of the participants on a team, with the goal of increasing the quality of every family interaction. Although the airlines have done an excellent job making sure families get what they need in times of crisis, it's still difficult for an ordinary employee to respond as effectively as a trained psychologist could. Future airline response teams may elect to retain trained psychologists who remain on standby as contract workers for the airline if a crash should occur. The psychologists could work throughout the year teaching sessions to airline volunteers to educate them on the larger emotional and philosophical issue of why such tragedies occur. An airplane crash is a catastrophic event, a tragedy much larger than the normal human or even the typical psychologist is likely to experience in his or her lifetime. Being able to reason and interpret the meaning behind it all is important before, during, and after working a crash activation.

An Emergency Response Team that consisted of trained mental health professionals would lessen risk, liability, and errors when working with families. It would show good faith on behalf of the airline that implemented it, because it would show a desire to diligently recruit qualified, trained professionals to perform one of the most important roles in the industry. Normal airline employees could manage the myriad administrative tasks at the crash-city location, and in outlying cities during the disaster response, but the sensitive task of dealing with the families who just lost their loved ones would be left to someone who had prepared for years for that very moment. It is now many years after Cali, and in my memory of the events during that time, I recall that many of the team members were young, like me, and for most it was their second or third year exposed to the corporate world. Although I was one of them, I still hold the belief that there can be no substitute for maturity and the evolution that comes with the progression of life. I did my best, but my ideal Emergency Response Team would be comprised of mature and experienced psychologists, social workers, and psychiatrists—team members who would be well equipped to meet the unique emotional needs of victims and their families.

* * *

Since the Cali crash, there have been many other tragedies in the world, and much has been written publicly about the airline industry, Emergency Response Teams, and the work the employees perform. In 2001, Nancy Chu, a survivor of American Flight 1420 that skidded off the runway in Little Rock, filed suit against the airline over her encounter with the Emergency Response Team member American assigned to her case after the crash.

Newspapers reported that although Nancy was lucky to survive, she received injuries that left her with brain damage, and in the months following the crash she embarked upon a journey of physical and emotional therapy. Prior to the crash, she had been a skilled sales assistant to a top-producing broker at an Arkansas Investment firm, but after the crash, her performance suffered, and she was demoted.

Jim Struthers, the baggage handler and Emergency Response Team member assigned to handle Nancy's case, urged Nancy to seek counseling for her trauma, and documented the events that transpired in his role as an Emergency Response Team member. His tasks included buying groceries and a caller ID box for Chu, and taking her to the hospital to visit a badly burned fourteen-year-old Chu had cared for at the crash scene.

But months later, Chu exposed their secret affair in court, alleging that the Emergency Response Team member had taken advantage of her, despite training that advised him of the vulnerability of crash survivors. He had been aware of the rules that forbid him from sustaining a personal relationship with a crash survivor while employed with the airline, but he had ignored them.

When Nancy Chu made the decision to board an airplane that day, she could not predict the consequence that was to follow, even though she had the same awareness as anyone about the inherent risks of flying. And when Jim Struthers made the decision to volunteer to participate on an Emergency Response Team, he had no idea that it would be a decision that would make headlines, and one that would change his life.

What happens when someone who has volunteered to serve on an Emergency Response Team is faced with a tragedy beyond imagination? The after effects are unknown, and perhaps it's better not to use volunteers at all.

After the events of 2001 and the multitude of airplane crashes and terrorist acts, police, fire, and airline crisis workers worked overtime. Those who volunteered to remain at the site of the World Trade Center for months after the tragedy can have no idea how they will be affected by the deep despair they witnessed on a daily basis. Some volunteers were quoted as saying they had returned home, but felt helpless sitting there in their own living rooms, so they returned to the site again. Restaurants closed for business, but remained open only to rescue workers. Normal citizens took months off from work to stay at the Trade Center and volunteer their time, handing out food and supplies. The day-to-day immersion in these tasks will have a lingering effect that will change their lives forever.

The events of September 11, when hijackers overtook four airplanes, resulting in the death of hundreds of passengers and thousands more on the ground, are inconceivable. It is a tragedy of higher proportion, one in which I cannot imagine having to explain or work through. I would not feel qualified to work with a family, to answer all of the questions they and everyone else in the nation would surely have in the minutes, hours, and days following the crash. The airlines have a tough challenge in operating such programs, and perhaps airlines will recognize this in years to come, and will set about the task of reorganizing the internal-response programs so that only trained experts may have continual, direct contact with the families and survivors of air disaster.

# chapter twenty-nine

# Finding Answers

Mercedes and I remain friends over the years, getting to know each other slowly, in small doses. Sometimes we meet in restaurants for lunch, other times we meet in corporate conference rooms for our organization for children, which is growing fast. When we meet over boxes of pizza in a donated conference facility, there are ten others with us, friends we've recruited as volunteers who dedicate their free time to help children in need.

Our group, which we have named Swingsets of the World, because of the playgrounds we'll be building, has already built three swingsets for children living in orphanages in Romania. In Texas, we have built two, and we have already worked in several homeless shelters, serving in other ways as well. We have served dinner to abandoned children, and we have arranged a weekend getaway for the caretakers of a children's home so that they can take time off to refocus and rejuvenate.

Mercedes and I have all but ignored the details of the accident, focusing instead on the things that tie us beyond the crash. We talk about the book I am writing, but in terms of how it is progressing, not the content itself. I have determined that both Mercedes and I are escapists; we will do anything to avoid what lies beneath. Mercedes is also altruistic and has a desire to honor her parents, so when we meet over lunch one day, I ask her if I can dedicate the book to her mother and father. Her eyes well up with tears. We agree that the book should be to honor them and the memory of everyone else that lost their lives that day.

Mercedes will contribute by sending me more stories about her parents, the two people who have had so much influence in shaping her life. We agree that the most comfortable way to do this will be via email, so that she can send me fragments of thoughts or whole stories as she remembers them. She laughs and warns me that she is not a great writer, but I have found the opposite to be true. Her writing is emotional and vivid, and through it I can envision the kind of people her mother and father were. Over the next several weeks, the emails from Mercedes trickle in. I set them aside until I am ready to be taken back to that time, because I know that my emotions will be stirred. Finally, three weeks after I receive them, I print the emails in the order in which they arrived and piece them together, reading them from a chair in a quiet corner of the house.

"Papi Papi ay viene el ice cream man!"

*I would run down the stairs and burst out the door as soon as I could hear the ringing bells of the ice-cream truck. As I tore through the door I would find my father sprinting across the yard in his tattered yard-work clothes towards the garage where he kept an old coffee can of spare change.*

*As soon as the ringing would begin down the street, my father knew I would soon be beckoning for his coffee-can contents, and he would always try to beat me to the punch. It was like a well-orchestrated baton-passing race. The bell rings, my father runs to the garage to get the change, and I book it to the truck before it had the chance to turn our corner. While he was rounding up enough change for me, he would run to the end of our driveway just to make sure I made it. My father knew exactly what made his seven-year-old daughter happy, and he would stop whatever he was doing to put a smile on my face. I always loved to spend time with my father.*

*My mother left for work—sanitation—by 5:30 every morning, so it was my father's responsibility to feed me and get me ready for the school day ahead. I would wake up cold in the midwestern winters, so my father would turn on the oven for me while I got ready. I'd go into the kitchen and change from my pajamas to my school clothes in front of the warm oven. My father, being the proper gentleman he was, would leave the room as soon as he saw me make my way towards the kitchen and let me get dressed. After getting dressed, my father would let me watch cartoons as I ate my daily bowl of cereal, and it was hard to tell who laughed the loudest during that hour. Me with Bugs Bunny, or my father with the Road Runner. My father found that cartoon a riot, and he would laugh like a child at the mischievous antics of the character.*

*In kindergarten, my mother had to cut my hair short, probably because my father had to take care of it every morning. Many times people thought I was a little boy because of my short hair, which my father had a hard time brushing through and styling. I was only five, and he was a man who had body slammed three hundred–pound men in front of thousands of screaming fans. It was probably a hard adjustment for him to take on such a domesticated role. But my father didn't give up, he allowed my hair to grow out and became a master of afro puffs, a hairdo involving one ponytail on each side of my head.*

*My friend Stacy, whom I've known since kindergarten, and Rich, a friend during college, will never let me live my afro puffs down, but as I look back at my school pictures and remember how my dad helped me get ready on those days, all I can do is lovingly smile.*

*Perhaps the best hairdo I ever had was in the second grade after my father decided to get fancy and sent me to class photos with my hair molded in a 1960s Mary Tyler Moore style. I remember it clearly. When he was finished I turned around to the mirror and was horrified. My father still had the bobby pins in his mouth and the brush in his hand, and he waited for my expression. Papi had spent an unusual amount of time on my hair that morning and I didn't want to hurt his feelings, so with a half-smile and a hug, all I could muster up to say was, "Gracias Papi."*

*I used to love working in the yard with my father in the fall. My parents always had a perfectly manicured lawn, so my father religiously spent hours on Saturday morning working on the yard. In the fall, my job was to help my father rake the leaves. I helped him rake in a yard that, at the time, seemed to be immense. After we'd rake them up into a few piles around the yard, we'd go around together pile by pile and pick the leaves up with two slats of wood into trash bags. In all honesty, we could have done the job in at least have the time, but I loved to turn my back to the piles and let myself fall into them, and each time my father laughed. So pile-by-pile I would play with my father, and it is a memory that is etched in my mind. Unfortunately, once I got to be in junior high school, I thought I was too old and too cool to help my old man out in the yard. What I wouldn't do to have another Saturday morning in the leaves with my father, without a care in the world.*

I set the stories aside in a file upon my desk. There are times in the ensuing months that I set about the task of writing and feel compelled to give up. After a solid week of this frustration and then another month of attempting to write more, I phone her.

"I'm having so many doubts about this book," I admit, exhaling deeply.

It is the first time I have confided my doubts to anyone, though the tension has been mounting for months. It's self-induced, but the questions continue to build in my mind. I am not an expert. I am not director of an aviation administration, and I am not a pilot. I am simply an ordinary person who was thrust into an extraordinary event. I have changed my mind about the program, and I'm not so sure about the value I myself provided the families of the crash victims. Airline employees are not counselors, and have no business working closely with those who have suffered a tragedy. How can I write an objective book when my views have become so cynical and my heart so soft? It was a random event, and a tragic one, yet I was merely a microcosm of it.

"Why are you having concerns?" Mercedes asks, her voice hushed and soothing.

"I just can't help but think of the what-ifs involved, and I keep wondering if the book will be worthwhile. Will it help anyone at all? I mean, at this point, it's all over, so what's the reason for writing it? I'm so frustrated by this whole thing."

"It will be a good book," she says firmly. "And a valuable one. So stop worrying about it. You know you're supposed to write it."

On the desk beside me is a photograph of Mercedes before the crash. She is standing with her parents wearing a white dress, her smile is innocent and sweet. Her mother wears a long strand of pearls and has the same identical poise about her. Her expression is regal, her smile disarming. Her father looks tall and elegant in a tuxedo, and his eyes stare straight into the camera. I lean back in my chair, mesmerized by their faces. A chill travels my spine and I realize that the book is a gift, and if it weren't the right thing to do, Mercedes would be the first to say.

"I wonder if your parents would like it?" I say. "Because when I write I am thinking of them, as if I am writing for them. I want it to be something they'd be proud of…"

"I'm sure they will be," she says reassuringly.

At this moment the seesaw tips again and it seems that the book is so *right*, as if her parents are looking down on us, urging it forward. It seems as if this has been orchestrated from the beginning.

"Thanks, Mercedes. You always know exactly what to say."

More than a year after we first meet, Mercedes invites me to dinner at her new home. I drive over on a Saturday night and park in front of the massive brick two-story with a golf-course view. I ring the bell, the door flies open, and before I know it a large Irish setter bounds out and jumps on me, wagging uncontrollably,

"Poo! Get down!" Mercedes says, summoning the dog inside.

The foyer is grand and circular, and a huge floral arrangement Mercedes has created adorns the entrance. Chris is in the kitchen preparing margaritas, a football game blares from the television. We eat at the dining-room table, which is long and formal, dining on steak and baked potatoes, my favorite meal. I have introduced her to a new companion, whom I had met in the years following my divorce, and as we sit around like four friends who have known each other a lifetime, I cannot help but think how extraordinary our friendship feels.

When I call her weeks later during my stopover in an airport in Chicago, we talk cell phone to cell phone for so long that my battery drains. Our conversations are no different than any others I have with girlfriends, and I ask about her job, the new promotion, and the people she works with. We talk for more than an hour until I realize what day it is.

"Happy birthday!" I say finally, and it is then that I wonder about the strain that had been evident in her voice. "Are you having a good day? Did I wake you?"

"No, I'm awake," she says softly.

Had she been crying? It was December 20, her *birthday*. But it is also the day of the crash. The date that her parents gave her life would forever be the same date that her parents died, though I am certain she does not see it that way.

"I'm just sitting here watching television for awhile," she adds. It is as if she can read my mind.

It is not a perfect world. There is tragedy all around and many more to come. There will be more survivors in the years ahead and more crisis workers called to respond to various tragedies across America. Some will make headlines for days and weeks, and though we do not yet know it, others will affect each of us so deeply, changing our generation and those before and after us, altering everything we ever knew. But I understand it now.

I will not disturb the other survivors who walked away from the mountain that day. They have all gone on with their lives. The experts had no professional or technical explanation for why only those who had been in the same row survived.

My journey to discover Mercedes has led me to a new under-standing of the tragedy that occurred that day, and I can now see the gift it has left behind for everyone touched by it. The ones who died on the airplane that day have been magnified, their legacy height-ened. Their children and grandchildren and the generations to follow will have a stronger appreciation for who they were, remembering the lessons they left behind. In a world where most people take legacy for granted, this tragedy has ensured that legacy will live on.

As our parents age, our connection to them becomes diluted over time and the things that were important to them get lost. We spend our energy rushing towards the future and forgetting about the past. We build our own traditions, our own laws within our own families, and it is not until our parents pass on that we realize something has been lost. This is something that Mercedes and I have been con-nected by, loss at an early age that provides us with a heightened sen-sitivity to the value of each day. She has become a whole person with a link to her past and a strong understanding of a heritage that she will pass on to her own children one day.

*   *   *

On a crisp December day six years after the crash, I wait for Mer-cedes at a steak house in Dallas where we have agreed to meet for lunch. I'm the first to arrive, and the hostess standing at a check-in desk beneath a stuffed deer directs me to a booth for two.

Mercedes is running late, on the heels of a hectic meeting that has obviously run over.

"I'm so sorry," she apologizes. "I had to come from across town."

"No problem at all."

Her long hair is clipped away from her face, allowing a wave of soft curls to fall down the back of her neck. She wears a tailored blue cot-ton shirt and black wool pants, a strand of white pearls hangs at her neck. She slides into the booth keeping both hands under the table.

"What's up?" I ask.

"Nothing…" she teases.

"So what's under the table?"

She grins and reveals a small gift bag she has been concealing.

"Here," she says, smiling. "This is for you."

"A Christmas gift?"

"Yes…just a little something that reminded me of you."

The bag is light, overflowing with colorful sheets of crinkled paper. It is a gift that has been carefully prepared.

"The package itself is a gift," I say. "It's beautiful."

"Open it! Open it!"

"Alright! Alright!"

I dig through the tissue paper until I find a blue velvet box containing an intricate clasp. I pry it open and reach for the fragile gift inside, a hand-blown glass ball with images of children holding hands. They are wearing traditional colors and clothes signifying various foreign countries, against the backdrop of the world. It is an image of many nations, diversity, and love. An image that seems to encapsulate our relationship and the reason we have been brought together.

"It's beautiful," I say, my eyes welling.

"When I saw it I thought of you instantly. It just reminded me so much of you."

"I love it, Mercedes. Thank you."

* * *

A year later, I am on a commercial flight home from Colorado, after a weekend away with my new husband, when, thirty minutes after takeoff, the airplane loses an engine.

In the moments that follow the aircraft lurches forward like a car running out of gas, and groans loudly. The cabin grows silent, and the passengers watch the panic in the flight attendant's eyes as she darts forward through the aisle, grabbing the emergency manual. My heart pounds wildly, and I stare out the window at the vast mountain range below, at the peaks that are dotted with trees jutting up from miles of dry, desolate valley. There is no one there to save us, and nowhere safe to land.

In the agonizing fifteen minutes that follow I wonder—is this how Mercedes felt? My mind races and I think of all the people that I love, and live for. There is nothing else to do. I do not know if we will live or die and I am powerless to change the course of fate. In that instant, and during the long, halted descent as we brace for an emergency landing, I realize that I know exactly what Mercedes had experienced in her own life. I understand that every decision we make no matter how small, has a consequence. But I also know that sometimes it's the decisions we don't make that can have the greatest impact on our lives. Who we are is the sum total of the positive and negative experiences that shape our lives. The trials are equally important as the victories—and whether we melt into cynicism after a tragedy or rise up to overcome it makes all the difference in who we become, and how we leave our legacy on the world.

# Flying Smart: Increasing Your Chances for Survival

During my long career in the airline industry and the years I served on the Emergency Response Team, I had time to reflect on what I would do in the event of disaster and how to prepare for one even before the airplane leaves the ground. After the hijacking of four airplanes on September 11, 2001, many Americans have done the same thing, contemplating the action they'd take if faced with a similar circumstance. Travelers and flight crew have taken a defensive stance, becoming their own air marshals who search the cabin for anyone or anything suspicious. In many ways this heightened awareness is positive for everyone; pilots have relied on passengers for years to point out mechanical failures the pilots themselves could not see from the cockpit. Engine fires, wing damage, or an unruly passenger are circumstances that a passenger is likely to see first.

Despite all that, terrorism is still a rare event in America, and an airplane crash due to other causes is far more likely. In just one year, 1997, two years after the accident in Cali, more than a thousand passengers died from a total of fifty-four plane crashes around the world. The primary cause of death from all crashes combined occurred not from the impact itself, but from the effects of smoke and fire inside the burning fuselage.

Since Cali, I've traveled thousands of airline miles in a quest to explore far corners of the world. But thinking in practical terms about what can happen if an airplane crashes could help save my life, and the lives of others, so I keep it in the back of my mind. When an airplane impacts, the resulting fire can ignite the fabric, seat cushions, and plastics inside the cabin and on the overhead bins. A cabin built for the comfort of passengers, with extended legroom and on-board movies, can suddenly be transformed into a burning inferno, where cumulative gas concentration develops, resulting in additional toxicity. The passengers trapped inside in search of an exit could be exposed to the lethal toxins that result in carbon-monoxide poisoning, which can occur as fast as one to two minutes after exposure, causing a quick and silent death.

In the confusion of a tragedy, the surge of adrenaline may make it impossible to feel the first warning signs of fatigue, nausea, or headache associated with deadly substances. Understanding this is key to survival, because several passengers have died in prior accidents helping others escape a smoky fuselage. In one accident, in 1991, in what seemed like a minor runway collision, a USAir 737 collided with a Sky West commuter plane on the ground in Los Angeles. The odds for survival were good because the collision occurred on the ground, not in the air, and the airplane was inside the airport fence with rescue vehicles and fire trucks readily available. Every passenger should have survived, but in the end there were thirty-four fatalities, eighteen of which were caused by smoke inhalation inside the fuselage. The bodies of a flight attendant and ten passengers were found within arm's length of the exit door. Later, a survivor reported that the exit door had been blocked for several crucial moments because two men fought over who would get out first. Tragically, passenger panic, combined with the smoke and toxins, created a deadly mix that all the safety procedures and aviation experts could not control.

In recent years, airlines and aviation organizations have spent millions on safety procedures and studies in order to decrease passenger deaths. Studies have focused on the post-impact escape efforts, toxins within the cabin, and time needed to evacuate to increase chances for survival. Aircraft manufacturers are now subject to specific standards and rules regarding the types of noncombustible materials used to make an airplane, and airlines must comply with these standards. Newer, noncombustible fabrics have been developed, and combustion toxicology studies using laboratory rats have been performed to determine the net effects of exposure.

Some studies measure the time it takes to become physically incapacitated as a result of the inhalation of toxic gas, since the inability to function occurs much earlier than death, and incapacitation ends the individual's escape efforts. The studies are ongoing, but several commercial carriers worldwide fly airplanes that were manufactured more than twenty-five years ago, so the outdated, combustible fabrics still exist. Flying smart is as simple as using the knowledge you've gained to make the small decisions that could affect your life, decisions many people never give a second thought. No one would invest their own money without doing research, yet most people make their personal travel decisions with cost as the top priority. We search the Internet for travel deals and click away until we've found the lowest possible fare. We disregard the size or financial status of the company, things we would most certainly investigate before placing our hard-earned incomes in a stock. We select the lowest round-trip fare and hope for the best, without doing any research at all.

Flying smart means changing basic behavioral tendencies and understanding that the point of booking is the first chance to make a decision for your personal safety. Know your company *before* you book; don't book with the fare as a priority. Has the airline turned a profit in the prior twelve months? If not, how much cash do you think they can allocate towards safety and maintenance? Is the carrier a small upstart that has inherited the aging fleet of other major airlines? Ask yourself if you want to fly on an airplane more than twenty-five years old, when other airlines have spent money on upgrading their fleet. Do your research, investigate annual reports, and take all of these factors into consideration *before* purchasing the ticket.

The average person tends to bundle all airlines together, when each company is actually very different, just like any other corporation. Most people won't choose a car frivolously, without carefully researching the previous performance of the manufacturer and the service the dealership provides its customers. The traveling public tends to speak of airlines with sweeping generalizations—"airlines are gouging us," "airfares are up"—yet airlines, just like other companies, are subject to investor scrutiny, profit and loss, and consumer demands.

An airline will survive or nose dive depending upon the experience and business acumen of its senior management. For the industry as a whole, safety and maintenance are a part of everyday business, but just like any other industry, some companies are better than others. Most airlines practice consistent and comprehensive safety and maintenance activities that ensure their travelers are safe, because the main product for any airline costs millions of dollars and man hours to maintain. If the aircraft fleet isn't in proper working order, the carrier has no product to sell.

Every carrier is required to operate under an established, predetermined maintenance program that includes several checks. Each aircraft has different parts, needs, and procedures for maintaining it, and each program is developed in concert with the airlines and the airplane manufacturer. Every plane arrives with a series of specific steps and actions required with regard to the aircraft's number of cycles, or takeoffs and landings.

For the major carriers, the maintenance program for a large jet involves inspection of the landing gear every three days, inspection of the exterior of the aircraft several times a day to look for leaks, worn tires, or other surface damage, and a weekly inspection of the control surfaces, auxiliary power systems, and other internal systems. While a visual check is part of the pilot's repertoire before every take-off, certified airplane mechanics inspect the aircraft daily and on an ongoing basis.

Inspections and safety procedures aside, it takes a lot of ingredients to make an airplane take off and land safely. There is no one specific factor that will make a plane safer or less safe, but several factors combined will. In all of my years in the airline industry the most frequent question I was asked is *Where is the safest place to sit on the airplane?* The airline industry has always been surrounded by a shroud of mystery, and it amused me when I was treated like a CIA agent privy to insider information that's hidden from the normal traveling public. *It's the exit row*, someone would say. *No, it's the tail section, because that's where the black box is*, others would insist.

The mystery surrounding airplane crashes and those who survive them have been the subject of debate for years, but the reality is that there is no one seat safer than the others. The main factors that can increase your chances for survival if an accident does occur are luck, prayer, and common sense. Evacuate quickly, get away from the plane, and don't roll on the ground to extinguish flames from your clothes unless there is no other option. After a crash, the ground can become soaked with jet fuel, igniting additional fires.

Wear something significant, in case an accident does occur, and make sure someone knows what it is before you go. Blue toenail polish? A significant watch? If a passenger is unconscious but clinging to life in a hospital in some strange city or country, he or she will be much easier to identify, so that family could be informed immediately. It may sound morbid, or be unpleasant to think about, but it's the smallest details that can have the largest impact. One of the most frustrating things I encountered during my time working a crash activation was the lack of call waiting in most of the households I attempted to contact. The phones would ring busy endlessly, until I had no other choice but to place that passenger's file under the bottom of the stack and move on to the next one. Inevitably, the next family's phone would ring busy, and though they were undoubtedly attempting to determine if their loved one had indeed been on the plane that crashed, their inbound calls to the airline would be met with frustration, because no information is given to an inbound caller. For security reasons, the passenger's emergency contact must be called by the airline, and only then can it be confirmed that the passenger had indeed checked in and boarded the plane.

Most passengers traveling domestically do not provide the airline with any emergency contact, so that when an accident does occur, the Emergency Response Team has no idea who to call. It's a simple thing to remember—at the time of booking, even if the reservation has been made via the Internet, contact the airline and provide them with an emergency name and telephone number. If an accident occurs, and if vital medical information is needed, your chances for survival will be greater.

FAA regulations require that every jet manufacturer must prove that an aircraft can be evacuated in ninety seconds. Airlines and jet manufacturers must conduct evacuation drills to prove it. This is a far leap from the embryonic days of aviation, when airlines and manufacturers worried about the act of flying itself. Early studies were focused on keeping the passengers alive while *in* the air, because aircraft design of early passenger jets was so rudimentary that the planes couldn't travel higher than ten thousand feet due to the lack of pressure in the cabin. Oxygen levels would be reduced to dangerous levels, disorienting passengers and causing them to faint. Motion sickness was a continual problem in the early days of flight until Boeing developed the Stratoliner, the first pressurized airplane.

Despite technical advances, a passenger's best defense after an impact is a proactive but intelligent attitude towards evacuation, and the knowledge that toxins can disable the central nervous system within minutes.

Although the preflight safety procedures given by the flight attendants focus on enabling oxygen masks and keeping the tray tables stowed during takeoff and landing, the fact is that when an airplane experiences a sudden impact, tray tables are bounced open, overhead bins disengage, and objects fly throughout the cabin. If the impact is severe, your seat belt may have been fastened but the entire seat could be projectiled through the air. Airplane seats and luggage and other contents from a cabin have been found miles from a crash site, in patterns that no flight attendant or safety procedure could have predicted.

Knowing where the available exits are on an aircraft and counting the specific number of rows to get to that exit are vital, but it is also critical to understand that many times the standard exits are broken or blocked, and the closest point of evacuation may not be the ones the flight attendants advised you of. Holes in the side of the airplane may be the best bet for evacuation, especially if the airplane has come to rest on its side and the exit door is blocked by the ground. If the plane impacts in a forest, the exits may be blocked by trees, but a small fire starting in an area of the fuselage may provide an opening for evacuation.

Flying smart means keeping your options open and staying tuned to your natural instincts for survival, but most of all, relax and have faith in an industry that is closely scrutinized by the FAA. Today's passenger jets are technically advanced, and many more people die annually from guns, drowning, and accidents around the home than from airplane crashes. The FAA monitors safety concerns and procedures that can avoid a crash and must approve every plane that is built, issuing an air-worthiness certificate that testifies that the aircraft has been constructed according to approved specifications.

Aeronautical engineers from the FAA are now part of the commercial aircraft design process and have also become heavily involved in the testing of prototypes. Not only must the commercial aircraft be sound, but every airline must pass a series of tests to earn the certificate that ensures that the airline has met a series of strict operation, maintenance, safety, and employee requirements. Although the airline industry is always the focus of intense criticism after a crash, it is also highly regulated, and one of the few industries in the world so completely dictated by safety.

Increase your odds for survival by choosing your carrier wisely and being aware of your surroundings at all times. It may sound amusing, but make minor changes in your life that will increase your health and athletic ability in any unforeseen circumstance you are placed in, and you can't go wrong. Stop smoking, start walking, and lose that ten pounds, that extra twenty pounds that has you huffing for air when you scale a flight of steps. In the end, it is common sense, and the work you have already done in your life, that prepares you for survival.

# About the Author

Tammy Kling is the author of *Searching for a Piece of My Soul,* which guides the reader through both the physical and emotional process of finding a long-lost relative or loved one. She has been featured on hundreds of national television and radio programs. She currently writes books from her farm in Dallas, Texas.